WHY
WHAT
HOW

Collecting Design
in a Contemporary Market

First published in 2010 by HSBC Private Bank

HSBC Private Bank (UK) Limited
8 Canada Square, London,
E14 5HQ, United Kingdom
www.hsbcpb.com

Edited and produced by Robert Violette, Violette Editions
www.violetteeditions.com

Design and art direction by Studio Frith
www.studiofrith.com

Picture research by Libby Sellers, Tamsin Perrett, Jo Walton
Copyedited by Stephen Patience
Editorial assistance by Stephanie Benjamin, Tamsin Perrett
Interviews transcribed by Bella Williams, George Charman
Digital retouching and repro by Violette Editions
Printed and bound in Italy by Graphicom

ISBN 978-0-9565766-0-6

A cip record for this book is available from the British Library.

The views and opinions expressed in this book do not necessarily
represent those of the publisher or its employees and affiliates.
Where the identity of a contributor is unknown or incomplete,
efforts have been made to identify and contact contributors.

Pages of this book are printed on recycled paper, made with
50–75% post-consumer waste or are printed on certified virgin
fiber (fsc and/or other standard).

HSBC Private Bank would like to express its deep gratitude to everyone who
has helped, through inspiration and hard work, in order to make this book a reality:
Libby Sellers, Robert Violette, Frith Kerr, Ben Prescott, Tamsin Perrett, Tony Joyce,
Alessandra Canavesi, Philippe Cathélaz and Maria Antonietta Potsios.

CONTENTS

PREFACE

One consequence of our so-called 'experience economy' has been a growing obsession with collecting possessions, memories and experiences in order to create personal histories, mementoes of our lives or simply to keep track of the immediate past. In tandem with this has been the increasing fortune of design as a cultural barometer and as a field of specialist collecting in its own right.

Over the last two decades, a wealth of new design galleries and dealerships have emerged from Shanghai to São Paulo, design fairs tailored specifically to the collector have launched, international auction houses have reformed their existing decorative arts sales into entire design departments, and prices for modern and contemporary designs are competitively surging. Driving this interest is a confluence of collectors, advisors and an increasingly sophisticated consumer seeking more from their surroundings than the everyday purchase. However, this is not just an externally driven phenomenon: for their part, designers have both initiated and responded to a market for unique, expressive and conceptual objects that push the boundaries of their industry. Given this extraordinary growth of interest in designed objects that go beyond what is ubiquitous and homogeneous, it seems apposite to acknowledge the history and contemporary position of the design collecting market.

WHY, WHAT, HOW offers a *bricolage* of theoretical, contextual and practical guidance for collectors of both historical and contemporary work, as well as for anyone interested in this particular sector of the much wider design industry. This book identifies the nuances separating the accumulated, everyday object from the collected, connoisseurial object, while highlighting some of the ambiguities that conflate the two. It charts key moments in design history from the last 150 years and illustrates important preoccupations shaping contemporary practice. It does not, however, seek to crystal-ball gaze or predict market trends. Instead this publication reviews what has come before and what is happening now to inform and inspire collectors.

In order to address these and other issues informing the contemporary market, this book has been devised in three sections: *WHY* – why the compulsion to collect and why we might collect design; *WHAT* – what is design and, consequently, what is collectible design; and *HOW* – an introductory guide to the processes and practicalities of acquiring and maintaining a design collection.

Interspersed are case studies that focus on a particular reading of important issues, such as the distinctions between the manufactured and the unique object or the influence of external factors in designating an object as collectible.

As a design curator and gallerist (some of the designers I work with are included in this book), my job in researching this book and in navigating the myriad of possible interpretations was greatly aided by the voices and opinions of designers, collectors and industry experts who have offered advice and tales from their own experiences. My sincere thanks go to Maarten Baas, Jurgen Bey, Janice Blackburn, Tony Chambers, Saskia Copper & Aad Krol, Tom Dixon, Ben Evans, Sjarel Ex, Patrik Fredrikson and Ian Stallard, David Gill, Steve Gourley, Rabih Hage, Jaime Hayón and Nienke Klunder, Heath Lambert/Blackwell Green Insurers, Brooke Hodge, Pierre Keller, Emily King, Brian Kisch, Reed Krakoff, Didier Krzentowski, Simon Lee, Arik Levy, George Lindemann, Julia Lohmann and Gero Grundmann, Peter Loughrey, Michael Maharam, Peter Marigold, Ambra Medda, Murray Moss, Marc Newson, Jay Osgerby, Alexander Payne, Yana Peel, Rodman Primack, Renny Ramakers, Alexander Ramselaar, Marc Rappolt, Alice Rawsthorn, Craig Robins, Mayer Rus, Zoë Ryan, Rolf Sachs, Matthew Slotover, Michael Smith, Sandra Smith, Casper Vissers, Cliff Williams and Jack Swabey, Gareth Williams, Alasdhair Willis and James Zemaitis.

I am also extremely grateful to the many designers, gallerists and auction house specialists who have not only been a guiding force but who have also generously lent images of the works illustrated. I am grateful to Tony Joyce and Alessandra Canavesi of HSBC Private Bank for initiating this publication, to Stephanie Benjamin for her assistance, and final thanks must go to Robert Violette and Studio Frith for their elegant and resourceful handling of the content and for producing a book that might one day be collectible in its own right.

LIBBY SELLERS, LONDON, MAY 2010

WHY

'WHAT,'
UTZ'S
MOTHER
ASKED
THE
FAMILY
PHYSICIAN,
'IS
THIS
MANIA
OF
KASPAR'S
FOR
PORCELAIN?'
'A
PERVERSION,'
HE
ANSWERED,
'SAME
AS
ANY
OTHER.'

CULTURES OF COLLECTING

Ever since the first vessel was made to carry water from the rivers of Mesopotamia, the development of objects has been inextricably linked with human evolution. However, the compulsion to collect objects – for both their functional and cultural value – is a far more affluent though marginally younger tale. The Roman emperor Augustus had his houses embellished not only with statues and pictures but also with objects which were curious by reason of their age and rarity, only for all these riches to be later pillaged by the Visigoths, Ostrogoths and Normans, all eager for the associated cachet such booty can bring. A less demonstrative sacking of Rome occurred again in the 15th century, when Renaissance nobility plundered the classical orders for inspiration, in order to build and furnish their palaces of power and culture.

From the *Kunstkammer* (art chamber) and *Wunderkammer* (cabinet of curiosities) of the Habsburg emperors to the souvenirs accumulated on the Grand Tours of 18th-century British aristocrats and 19th-century robber barons alike; from the institutional collections established from private donations at the turn of the 20th century to the maharajahs of the early 20th century and the great European decorators of the interwar period, the appreciation of objects and their perceived power to imbue vestiges of enlightenment and prestige is millennia old.

With these engaging dialogues between collectors and their possessions came an urge – among philosophers, historians, ethnographers, social scientists and literary critics – to analyse this compulsion to collect. Driven by obsession, competition or simply just to fill a void (functional or otherwise), collecting is often seen as a pathological attempt to exert control over our environment and to memorialise, if not completely hinder, the passing of time. As both malady and remedy, our relationship to objects has been the subject of Freudian psychoanalysis and Marxist ideology. Sigmund Freud, a collector himself, noted in 1938, 'a collection to which there are no additions is really dead.' Among Walter Benjamin's case studies, the collector occupies a privileged place. For him collecting involves the retrieval and ordering of things past: 'Every passion borders on the chaotic but the collector's passion borders on the chaos of memories:'[2] collections were mnemonic treasure houses, recalling the circumstances in which an object was acquired.

WHY

In her study *On Collecting*, museologist Susan Pearce[3] identifies three types of collection:

The Souvenir: an intensely personal or 'curious' collection, perhaps amassed by an individual during their lifetime, which has memory and trace associations with its production, accumulation, purchase or use; often thought of in museo-logical terms, if not actually to be donated to a museum.

The Systematic: an academic approach to collecting, whereby the objects represent principles of organisation that are scientifically verified via observation and study: the classic, one-of-every-kind approach.

The Fetishistic: objects that are 'artful' or 'magically active' collected by 'people whose imaginations identify with the objects they desire to gather.'

Collections of popular culture – such as the mouthpieces of musical instruments, Italian fishing lures, 'wheat' pennies produced before 1945 – perhaps fit Pearce's last category, while connoisseurial collections – the focus of this book – typically occupy the first two.

What unites these treatises is the shared belief that every collection is a reflection of its owner. The analogy of collection as mirror is perfect, precisely because it sends back not real images, but desired ones. No collection can be objective. It is in the nature of collecting that it is based on individual choices. What category of things to collect is one key choice; which pieces to focus on is another. Unerringly, these choices will reveal the personality behind the collection.

I suppose what I love about collecting – and I suppose this is the real thing about collecting – is what it teaches you about yourself. The way to do it is to buy things that appeal to you, because the thing that links them all is you, of course.

Matthew Slotover, director, Frieze, London[4]

I THINK PEOPLE COLLECT LIBRARIES
BECAUSE WHAT THEY'RE TRYING TO DO
IS ILLUSTRATE WHAT'S IN THEIR BRAINS:

THEIR LEARNING CURVE,
THEIR EDUCATION,
THEIR LEANINGS,
THEIR BIASES,
THEIR PREJUDICES,
THEIR INTERESTS,
THEIR DEPTH.

AND I THINK THAT THAT WOULD BE THE SAME –
ALTHOUGH CERTAINLY
THERE'S A BULK ISSUE – WITH OBJECTS.
I THINK IF WE LOOK AT IT LIKE THIS,
AS INANIMATE OBJECTS THAT ARE SOUVENIRS
IN THE TRUE FRENCH ORIGINAL SENSE
OF THE WORD SOUVENIR –
TO REMEMBER,
TO REMIND US,
AND ALSO TO PROJECT
– IT'S A WAY OF DEFINING WHO WE ARE,
WHAT OUR EVOLUTIONARY THINKING HAS BEEN,
AND WHO WE'D LIKE TO BE.

WHY

Recently I have taken to acquiring what is known as a 'significant' collection, meaning a complete exhibition… the idea of possessing the event… an exhibition is thought out as an ensemble, but if we buy only one or two pieces, we lose the event of the ensemble. Finally, owning an ensemble is also a means of marking time.

Marcel Brient, collector, Paris [5]

As the radical French philosopher Jean Baudrillard noted in his seminal 1968 text *The System of Objects*, among the various meanings of the French word *objet*, the Littré dictionary gives this: 'Anything which is the cause or subject of a passion; figuratively and *par excellence* – the loved object.' [7]

Collecting the loved object – for all its psychoanalytical connotations with self-love – is a passion, and one that pushes the boundaries and resources of even the most endowed collector. It's a compulsion or a bug that, once caught, is very difficult to shake, and can offer whole new worlds of pleasure. The collectors who get the most out of this experience are those for whom the objects bring joy and enrichment to their lives.

For the most part, collectors of design are seeking something that goes beyond the readily available, wanting an extra something from the objects they choose to surround themselves with. However, there are so many subjective reasons and influences that can tip an object from being simply functional to being both functional and desirable.

Baudrillard continues: 'Our ordinary environment is always ambiguous: functionality is forever collapsing into subjectivity, and possession is continually getting entangled with utility.' [8]

Ambiguity is the key point here; each of us admires the quotidian – the stuff of daily life – in entirely different ways. Each of us brings our own set of values to the object. The same idea could never be applied to collecting art, as there is no conversation about functionality and utility in art. Yet it is exactly this ambiguity – this dual role, this blurring of the subjective and objective – that makes design particularly alluring to collectors.

Philippe Starck, the media darling of French Postmodernism, offered the perfect example through the triffid-like aluminium Juicy Salif lemon juicer he designed for the manufacturer Alessi in the late 1980s.

Described as a parvenu's gewgaw – more cultish totem than juicer – it is particularly bad at juicing lemons, but nevertheless found its way onto many middle-class kitchen counter tops and became one of Alessi's top-selling products. Starck has since acknowledged the failures of the Juicy Salif and has instead claimed that its true success, its true function was as a talking point: 'My juicer is not meant to squeeze lemons; it is meant to start conversations.'[9] The fact that such a supposedly humble object (and one that failed its practical purpose so miserably) was proudly kept on display is part of its mythology.

In addressing these ambiguities, we must also address what is meant by collectible design. For the purposes of this book, it is not wheat pennies, mouthpieces or Starck's juicer (although they say much about the owners' fascination with history and form), but objects that attain an accepted connoisseurial status. The point at which this status changes – particularly in relation to objects that were mass-manufactured and never intended to be 'collectible', or to hold value beyond their functional one – is equally ambiguous.

Much post-industrial and all Modernist design (pertaining to the architectural and design movement that flourished in Europe after World War I) was not created for private collections. It was not the preserve of the individual, but designed for the masses. In the Modernist world, celebrating the unique was a contradiction in terms (see 'Modernist Goals?' p. 27). This is not to say it didn't happen, but celebrating the individual at the exclusion of the everyman was not part of design's politicised agenda at that time.

The French architect and designer Jean Prouvé's experiments with new folded-steel technologies in the 1920s and 1930s led to a series of chairs, tables and furniture arrangements, originally designed for the public sector in the growing areas of health, education and administration. His avoidance of the domestic market reflected a social ideal, but larger orders also offered economies of scale. By 1934 he had a commission for 800 pieces of office furniture for the headquarters of the Paris power company CPDE. One secondary school in Metz ordered 1,000 items, including beds, chairs and desks. These successes led his company, in 1936, to produce a catalogue of standard models for hospitals, schools and offices.

Jean Prouvé
Amphitheatre *banquette*,
Faculté de lettres, Besançon, 1953

That these designs by Prouvé – a legendary figure in design and architectural history – were made in relative quantity is one reason why they are now so collectible on a secondary market: examples surface regularly enough to maintain the attention of collectors who wish to be part of the Prouvé club. Ironically, they were ideologically conceived to be the very opposite; it is this notion – that they were created with such a socially inclusive, moral purpose – that makes these designs appeal on an intellectual and scholarly level to individual collectors.

Beyond the personal or critical valuations, there is obviously a strong incentive for collecting something that might accrue in market value. The enrichment here might not be emotional, but financial (though the two aren't always mutually exclusive).

It's an emotional investment, but you want your emotions validated by finances. You want the finances to match your emotional investment.

Mark Rappolt, editor, *Art Review* [10]

The reasons why any one object might increase in value or be considered collectible are many. It could be that:

- The work was designed at a pivotal or evolutionary moment of a successful career and it marks this moment

- The work is by an influential or celebrated designer and/or is rare (due to limitations on its manufacture or that the existing examples do not get put back on the market)

- The circumstances surrounding the work's origins may have some significant historical association, e.g. The Festival of Britain in 1951

- The designer's death has led to the cessation of further production

- The work employs highly complex and atypical technologies, processes or materials that elevate it beyond existing forms

- The work is an expression of a particularly interesting and important socio-economic or political period

- The work relates to a larger architectural or institutional power that imbues the design with a layer of 'scholarly' approval

- The work was the prototype to a successful edition or manufactured series

External catalysts could include:

- The design has recently been featured in an auction or exhibition, endorsing the validity of the work

- This exhibition or auction 'rediscovered' an overlooked design or designer, bringing their value back into context

- The work has been re-contextualised in that exhibition or sale, due to either the curatorial/market agenda or its basic physical placement beside other works

- The works had been held back by galleries and dealers who were waiting for the right moment to release them back into the market

- Another major collector or influential figure has publicly endorsed the work by making their purchase known, either through a magazine feature on their home or collection, or by being witnessed purchasing the piece

- The works have an added allure from being part of a famous collection, e.g. the Yves Saint Laurent and Pierre Bergé collection auctioned by Christie's in Paris, February 2009

People generally have a pretty good idea of what's decent now. Differentiating the good from the great becomes the big challenge, which is what propels people to collect classics. I think that's what drives people to collect things that have an enduring value. That's the majority of people. Then you have the minority of people who are willing to bet on what might have the enduring value.

Michael Maharam, director, Maharam, New York

The rationale that might lead a collector towards design are equally varied:

- A respect or interest in technological or material innovation, as expressed through objects

- To preserve either an historical moment or to capture the essence of now

- The cachet of owning a celebrated, rare or unique object

- As part of the poetic through which individuals define themselves

- The potential financial incentives

- To invest in objects that have the same cultural or financial capital as an existing art collection

- For the thrill of the chase, and the competition such a chase can bring

- For the kudos and social allure of being part of a relatively niche group of like-minded collectors

- To be a patron of culture

◔ To have objects that have been designed with consideration for their added narrative or cultural value as opposed to simply having a functional use

Just as a museum curator follows an acquisition policy and assesses the value of a work before committing to it, so too do many collectors. It is a consideration of output, value and the contribution this designer or object has made to contemporary culture – and why it should form part of their collection. While many collectors of design buy an object to serve its intended purpose, increasingly collectors are acquiring works with an agenda that goes beyond the needs of functionality or interior decoration. This reflects an appreciation of design's dual role as both functional item and a vessel for subjectivity. It also is symptomatic of the changes coming from within the industry, the growing tendency for design to be used as a reference about the industry – a comment on its own production, or its own environment. This often leads to works that are less functional, more theoretical in their output.

The design market is much more academic in the main. Art is driven by status, design by enthusiasts. If you spend six figures for a side table that no one but you knows what it is really about, then you have to really love it for itself.

Reed Krakoff, collector, New York [12]

Collectors have been working with cutting-edge architects and designers and decorators to make places for their art collections, and there seemed to be room in these environments for furniture and things that blur the line between furniture and sculpture. There seemed to be a personal connection to a lot of the material that eased this transition or this elevation of design out of a pure design ghetto and into a more mainstream art context.

Mayer Rus, design editor, *LA Times* [13]

OBVIOUSLY
THERE ARE SOME
VERY CULTURED COLLECTORS
WHO HAVE DONE THEIR HOMEWORK
AND ENTER A SYMBIOTIC CONVERSATION
ABOUT WHERE THEIR COLLECTION IS GOING.
BUT THERE ARE SOME OTHERS THAT,
PARTICULARLY AT THE EARLY STAGES,
JUST WANT TO LEARN WITH YOU.
THEY
GROW
WITH
YOU
AND IN THE END
THEY BECOME EVEN
BIGGER EXPERTS
THAN YOU ARE,
UNAVOIDABLY.
AND
I THINK THAT PASSAGE
IS ACTUALLY
VERY EXCITING.

PEOPLE
TEND TO THINK
DIFFERENTLY ABOUT OWNING
ART TO OWNING DESIGN, BECAUSE
YOU OWN DESIGN ANYWAY, IN ALL THE
OBJECTS YOU HAVE AROUND YOU. UNCON-
SCIOUSLY YOU ARE COLLECTING THE MINUTE
YOU BUY ANYTHING. THE BIG DIFFERENCE IS
HOW YOU EVOLVE THOSE DECISIONS IN TERMS
OF WHAT YOU BUY: YOU'RE SPLIT BETWEEN BEING
INTERESTED IN THE ACTUAL MANUFACTURE OF
ORDINARY OBJECTS AND THE PSYCHOLOGY OF
COLLECTING MORE EXPENSIVE VERSIONS OF
THOSE OBJECTS. WHAT'S BEEN INTERESTING
TO US IS EXACTLY WHERE THAT BOUNDARY
LIES. I THINK THE EXCITING THING ABOUT
DESIGN WOULD BE THAT DOESN'T HAVE
THAT KIND OF 'WHITE-CUBED
ART' THING: IT'S MORE
ACCESSIBLE.

People want to categorise things, process things into a category. Perhaps they don't have the tools to make a decision or trust their instinct. My personal preference would be to combine the historical and the contemporary, as we can't see the world in one view.

Ambra Medda, director, Design Miami/ [15]

There are many different kinds of collector: the prosperity collector, the posterity collector, the academic collector, the patron and the accidental collector – someone who has stumbled into collecting by virtue of being curious and wanting to furnish their home with objects that go beyond the everyday and the ubiquitous.

And herein lies another ambiguity with design. Is it correct to say we are collecting it if the object's purpose is to be used, or if its purchase follows no methodical rationale? Is purchasing a rare item or seeking something with collectible status qualifiedly collecting, if it is to become part of the furniture? This book does not seek to make such judgements; instead it assumes that anyone interested in purchasing rare items is interested in both sides of this subjective investment in design. By raising the question, however, the book hopes to draw the collectors' attention to the possibility of appreciating design for its many other valuable virtues.

For many creatives, the reason for working in design is that it is connected to the real world. The constraints of designing something for use – be it a chair, street signage or a vase – are what compel them forward, to find solutions through the language of process and materials.

In this sense, we are all 'collectors' of design – it infiltrates our every waking moment: from the alarm clock that reminds us to pick up the toothbrush, through the clothes selected to get us out the door in order to navigate the complex systems of transport and signage, to the infrastructures that facilitate work, the advances in technology that keep our health regulated, the ease with which our children access educational facilities, and the systems that enable us to operate our daily lives.

But not all of the categories that fall under the large umbrella of 'design' are the types that might be actively pursued, for whatever purpose, as collectible design.

WHAT
I LOOK FOR IN
CONTEMPORARY DESIGN
IS THAT KIND OF TIMELESSNESS
THAT ENABLES YOU TO LIVE WITH
THE PIECE BEYOND
ITS SCULPTURAL
VALUE.

ART
DOESN'T NEED TO
FUNCTION BUT DESIGN DOES, SO
I CAN LOOK AT SCULPTURE AND
APPRECIATE THAT BUT FOR ME,
A TABLE NEEDS TO BE USED AS
A TABLE EVEN IF IT HAS
50 YEARS OF SCULPTURAL
LEGACY BEHIND
IT.

THERE ARE THREE COMPONENTS TO COLLECTING:
COLLECT
WHAT YOU LIKE,
COLLECT
WHAT MAKES YOU MONEY,
OR
COLLECT
THE OVERLAP.
OF COURSE,
YOU WOULD HOPE THAT PEOPLE WOULD COLLECT THE OVERLAP. IN THE WORST-CASE SCENARIO, SOMETHING'S GOING TO BE COLLECTED BECAUSE IT'S GOING TO MAKE YOU LOTS OF MONEY, OR IT'S RELIABLE. BEST-CASE SCENARIO IS THE OVERLAP, AND PERHAPS AN INVESTOR'S WORST-CASE SCENARIO IS ONLY COLLECTING WHAT YOU LIKE. YOU BUY WHAT YOU CAN AFFORD TO BUY. AND IF YOU WANTED TO SPLIT IT A DIFFERENT WAY, BUY THE BEST OF WHAT YOU CAN AFFORD TO BUY. WONDERFUL. OR BUY LOTS OF LITTLE THINGS. IF THAT PLEASES YOU, FINE. FROM AN INVESTMENT PERSPECTIVE, YOU'RE ALWAYS GOING TO BE BETTER OFF BUYING THE BEST QUALITY OF WHAT YOU CAN AFFORD TO BUY.

I
CREATE
RULES
FOR
MY
COLLECTING,
WHICH
I
BREAK
ALL THE TIME,
BUT THE
OVERRIDING
RULE
THAT
I
DON'T BREAK,
IS
'IS THIS
GOING TO MAKE
ME
HAPPIER?'

MODERNIST GOALS?

CASE STUDY

Since the beginning of this century, since the rise of the design fair, auction house and gallery market that, through its very nature, challenges the widely held and Modernist-led tenet that design should only be for mass consumption, concerns have been strongly voiced about the threat this market poses to design in general. A handful have described it as the 'death of design', while others – threatened by the high prices, controlled quantities and seemingly non-functional appeal of some the works – have accused design of mimicking art. The debate played out across the blogosphere and through countless print articles has largely been a media construct, with words such as 'design art' applied to the work with a sneer of contempt and disdain, and the term always presented in quotation marks. Those against argue that this market has actively ignored the revolutionary advances of design's ability for positive change and replaced the Modernist ideal with elitist, meretricious objects, a superfluous use of increasingly scant resources and concepts that serve no purpose other than to internalise design's agenda. The debate has polarised the industry, but it is partially predicated on an exceptionally restricted appreciation of the industry, its historical limitations and subsequent development.

It is undeniable that marketing design in this manner – through galleries and auction houses – has strengthened over the last decade, but the goal of creating pieces that either celebrate uniqueness or are limited by their own virtuosity is not new. Perhaps a more appropriate description might be 'renewed', for there exist many parallels between what is happening now and other significant moments in design history.

The Arts and Crafts movement of the late Victorian period was also criticised for attracting the attention of a wealthy clientele. It emerged at the beginning of a serious economic recession and towards the end of a century in which efforts were being made to address what was seen as the devastating effects of industrialisation on the design and manufacture of goods. It was never suggested, implicitly or otherwise, that machine production and commercial manufacture were the enemy or that they should be abandoned. Instead the movement sought to elevate the status of the craftsman and give due recognition to the individual through a reappraisal of the applied arts' role in society.

This liberal approach saw like-minded patrons commission entire environments – fine art, architectural features and exquisite bespoke furnishings made by both machine and hand – with consideration for the gestalt, or the unified whole.

Even the French Modernists, the arbiters of machine manufacturing and standardisation, created objects to be marketed and sold through small editions or that were beyond the capabilities of their contemporary manufacturing technologies. As the designer Tom Dixon notes: 'There has always been a tradition of making small quantities for a select group of people, whether that was the big designer-decorators of the 1930s working for maharajahs, or even the Modernists like Le Corbusier… despite the theory that it was machine-industrial production, it was effectively made like jewellery; it was one-offs by highly specialised people that were experimenting and innovating in new materials or new technologies long before it earned mass appeal. I was speaking to Charlotte Perriand's daughter about the most famous, iconic piece of Modernist design: the "B306 chaise" that Perriand designed with Le Corbusier and Pierre Jeanneret in 1928. It sold only 12 pieces pre-war. In their minds it was definitely intended for machine production, but in reality, it was a sort of luxury item which had a very small market.'[20] That they barely sold was not to do with intention but with taste, and the lack of appeal to manufacturers geared to pre-war bourgeois style and the culturally ingrained aesthetics of comfort.

Among the most important designers and architects of the early 20th century, Eileen Gray (1878–1976) was arguably the most influential woman to practise in those fields. Despite this acclaim, Gray's achievements went unrecognised for most of her lifetime. Her surviving works are rare, and the few original items that perpetuate her collectability were actually designed during an early period in her career before she was championing Modernist idioms. Gray was awkward to pigeonhole, making it hard for either her work or her enormous potential to be recognised. As a woman working in a male-dominated sphere, a self-taught practitioner and an Irish expatriate living in France, she does not fit the mould of important 20th-century designers.

Reticent to the point of reclusive, she lacked the impetus to develop the personal myths vital to the cult of individual architects. When her work was first presented in 1972 in an auction hosted by Camard, Paris, few knew that Gray was alive, let alone still living in her apartment in rue Bonaparte, hard at work at the age of 94. When Jean-Pierre Camard showed Gray a photograph of the 'Lotus' table she had made for the couturier Jacques Doucet, c. 1913, the designer reacted badly. 'I don't recognise it,' Gray said. 'It is shameful to have done that.' Camard was rightly thrown and asked, 'What do you mean, you don't recognise it?' It turned out that she objected to the silk cords and amber baubles Doucet had added to her table. 'I want you to destroy it,' she told Camard. The table sold for 61,000 francs. When Camard told Gray on the telephone, she replied: 'It doesn't mean it's good. It means it's expensive. That's all.'[21] The Camard sale initiated a market reappraisal of Gray's outputs which, as James Zemaitis of Sotheby's has noted, 'was at the same time that Art Deco as a cultural phenomenon was also being rediscovered. With two exhibitions in the US in the early 1970s, with collectors such as Yves Saint Laurent, a young Karl Lagerfeld, and a 20-year-old Peter Brant all buying into Art Deco … it was all happening at the same time.'[22]

Eileen Gray
Dragon chair
1917–19

CASE STUDY

31

When serious academic rehabilitation came in 1973 in the form of an exhibition at the Royal Institute of British Architects, Gray declined to attend the opening, preferring to view the exhibition in private. A flurry of newspaper articles and official honours followed, drawing interest from commercial manufacturers in Paris and London alike. In 1973, the London-based manufacturer and retailer Zeev Aram negotiated licensing rights to a number of Gray's designs, and she lived just long enough to see some of her furniture put into production, half a century after it was designed.

For design and architecture historians, Gray's work was correspondingly awkward: it could never be shoehorned into the neat narratives of 20th-century design and architecture. Earlier pieces such as the 'Dragon' chair (which sold in 2009 for a record-breaking £19 million in the Christie's auction of Yves Saint Laurent's private collection) or the 'Lotus' table, being both luxurious and modern, appear typical of Art Deco, yet Gray was working in that idiom years before Art Deco had even hit its stride in the mid-1920s.

When she turned her back on such youthful exoticism, it was to embrace the strictures of Modernism. Gray, however, did not fit comfortably into that movement either. A guiding tenet of Modernism was an almost utopian belief in the power of technology, often resulting in a crude celebration of the machine. The tag of functionalism, for example, was applied to chairs that looked technically advanced but came with no guarantee of functional comfort. Gray was not easily co-opted, and while her work looks utterly modern, her aesthetic was dedicated to the physical and psychological comfort of the user. She wrote what must have seemed almost heretical at the time: 'Modern designers have exaggerated the technological side.' Instead, in the furniture and spaces she designed she tried to ensure that the individual was the primary consideration.

The same singularity of vision, which makes her work so inspiring and celebrated today, had served to relegate Eileen Gray to obscurity for much of her career.

With the mid-century designers whose reputations have enjoyed such staggering success in the last five or 10 years, it's also to do with a reappraisal of the mid-20th century in general in terms of its architecture, literature, film, culture, and politics. You could extend that argument to thinking it was actually a post-Cold War reappraisal of that time which was enabling figures to come through. In the case of Eileen Gray, it's also to do with a critical reappraisal of work by women. With such a neglected figure, it becomes a kind of vacuum that forces can flow into and fill that cup up.

Gareth Williams, Senior Tutor of Design Products at
the Royal College of Art, formerly Curator of 20th-century
and contemporary furniture at the V&A, London[20]

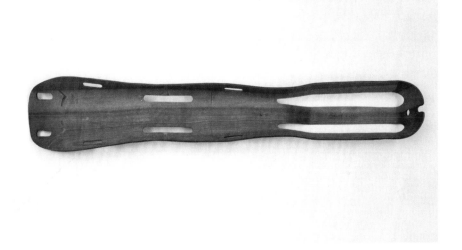

Charles & Ray Eames
Leg splint
1942

Charles and Ray Eames, the American husband-and-wife team who are often cited as exemplars of democratic design, were, like Charlotte Perriand, beset by the shortcomings of industrial manufacture. In the early 1940s they were producing prototypes – made using wood and glue 'borrowed' from Charles' day job as a set designer for MGM – from a home-made moulding machine in the back room of their Los Angeles home. A series of chairs (co-designed with Eero Saarinen, a colleague from the Cranbrook Academy) featured moulded-plywood shells covered with foam-rubber padding and upholstery fabric. Eames had wanted to join the legs to the shell using cycle welding, but was unable to do so because the process was restricted to military applications during the war.

Their organically shaped 'La Chaise', inspired by Gaston Lachaise's 1927 sculpture *Reclining Nude*, was designed in 1948 for the Museum of Modern Art's international competition for low-cost furniture design.

Ironically it proved too expensive to manufacture at the time, and only went into production in 1990 and has been produced in small quantities ever since. In an article about modern furniture, George Nelson (along with the Eameses, one of the founders of American Modernism) writes, '[The] postwar yearnings for a new innocence and simplicity [were] often reflected in furniture that reached for a primitive quality but achieved, as often as not, a fair degree of sophistication.'[24]

The way histories are narrated, the emphasis on certain individuals or movements (to the detriment of others), the political or social agendas behind these movements and the availability of source material all affect the provenance of a designer's work. Modernism – for all its highly conscientious and valid aspirations – was not as utopian in practice as history would have us believe. This does not excuse or justify superfluity in contemporary design – but must have some bearing on how we judge it and what tools we use to do so.

Charles & Ray Eames
La Chaise
1948

CASE STUDY

35

WHAT

IN MOST PEOPLE'S VOCABULARIES,
DESIGN MEANS VENEER.
IT'S INTERIOR DECORATING.
IT'S THE FABRIC OF THE CURTAINS OF THE SOFA.
BUT TO ME, NOTHING COULD BE FURTHER
FROM THE MEANING OF DESIGN.

...DESIGN IS THE FUNDAMENTAL SOUL OF A HUMAN-MADE CREATION...

THAT ENDS UP EXPRESSING ITSELF IN SUCCESSIVE
OUTER LAYERS OF THE PRODUCT OR SERVICE.

Design is unique among the creative disciplines in that the word refers both to what practitioners do, and to what they produce. Composing, painting and writing are used to describe the act of creation, while music, art and literature are the corresponding results. However design, as design historian John Heskett has written, 'is to produce a design to design a design.' As both a verb and noun, design is too indiscriminate to accommodate the wealth of activities and the subsequent results that designers produce. Yet when used as an adjective, as in 'designer hotel', it implies certain inherent qualities that differentiate the 'designed' object from everything else, adding value through the suggested hand of the maker.

This appreciation for authorship has been a catalyst for some of the changes in design – its production, marketing and consumption – over the last few decades. It has been both fed and fuelled by a growing media, led by the cult of celebrity and eager for photogenic content, and by industry's need to perpetuate interest and generate new content to feed this media and an increasingly sophisticated (though over-saturated) consumer market. However, in humanising design – by putting a face to the person behind the object, design has also become less alienating and more personable. The designer has been able come out from behind the big green curtain of Oz and engage with Dorothy – no longer a nameless cog in the greater machine aesthetic, but able to nurture relationships with the design's end users.

Nevertheless, the adjectival excesses of the 1980s – the 'designer decade' – debased the term design; it became a marketing conceit meaning nothing more than that the item had been conceived of by someone (usually anonymous) and was therefore permissibly more expensive or desirable. As a result, many firms and individuals distanced themselves from the term in fear of being misconstrued as 'stylists', or that their efforts were restricted to how things looked. In their valid reactions against this particularly late 20th-century misappropriation of the term, they were inadvertently promoting the much earlier 20th-century, puritanical understanding of design.

To the Modernist architects and designers working in Europe between the wars, design was a moral undertaking with a clear, left-leaning social agenda: to harness mass-production in order to provide affordable, functional objects that would improve the quality of life. Through their deployment of the credo 'form ever follows function', anything that did not display functional rigour, or which flirted with decoration, was relegated to the minor category of decorative arts (or, worse, 'style'), and therefore best avoided for fear of moral or aesthetic corruption.

For its faith in technological progress and its actual advances in design production and material manipulation, Modernism is worthy of the praise it generates. In retrospect, however, the Modernists' stated agenda cannot be read as anything other than an aesthetic imposed from on high. However much they derided 'style' as bourgeois and profligate, the Modernists could be considered among the most doctrinaire stylists in design history. Given our contemporary advances in Computer Aided Design (CAD) and Computer Aided Manufacture (CAM) the Modernists' 'machine aesthetic' also now seems redundant, as much of the machinery used to produce design today is invisible.

A contemporary understanding of design most definitely includes an appreciation of how an object looks: as Charles Eames once said, 'the details are not the details. They make the design.' Alongside its form, its use of materials, and how it was made, is a wealth of intangible drivers: economy, politics, popular culture and marketing. This ambiguity was perhaps best phrased in 2001 by communication designer Erik Adigard: 'Design is in everything we make, but it's also between those things. It's a mix of craft, science, storytelling, propaganda, and philosophy.'[26]

The function of art is to make you reflect, to make you see, open a new window on the world, to expand your thoughts, your beliefs, to transform the world around you. I think design has the same or could have the same ability to do that whilst still fulfilling another, very practical function.

Julia Lohmann, designer, London[27]

The traditional demarcations between disciplines have receded, and designers are increasingly marketing themselves not by just a visual language that they create but how they structure and manage their design process. That all plays a role in how we speak about design. It's not just about problem-solving. We really are seeing it much more as a creative endeavour, whether it's a purely abstract form of self-expression or whether it's trying to address underlying principles of society. For example, work that's created with meaning and responsibility, that addresses the entire life-cycle of an object, as well as the emotional well-being of the user. These issues that are quite often sidelined in the digital era.

Zoë Ryan, Neville Bryan Curator of Design,
Art Institute of Chicago[23]

PRINCIPLES

In this sophisticated consumer age, the polarities of good design and bad design are no longer valid; instead it is a dialogue between good and better design. What has always determined this, regardless of era, is taste: a nebulous concept shaped by experience, education, economics and context.

In a book titled *What is Modern Design* published in 1950, New York's Museum of Modern Art sought to explain the principles of good design to post-war consumers in a 12-point checklist composed by the museum's curator, Edgar Kauffman Jr:

- Modern design should fulfil the practical needs of modern life

- Modern design should express the spirit of our times

- Modern design should benefit by contemporary advances in the fine arts and pure sciences

- Modern design should take advantage of new materials and techniques and develop familiar ones

- Modern design should develop the forms, textures and colours that spring from the direct fulfilment of requirements in appropriate materials and techniques

- Modern design should express the purpose of an object, never making it seem to be what it is not

- Modern design should express the qualities and beauties of the materials used, never making the materials seem to be what they are not

- Modern design should express the methods used to make an object, not disguising mass-production as handicraft or simulating a technique not used

- Modern design should blend the expression of utility, materials and process into a visually satisfactory whole

- Modern design should be simple, its structure evident in its appearance, avoiding extraneous enrichment

- Modern design should master the machine for the service of man

- Modern design should serve as wide a public as possible, considering modest needs and limited costs no less challenging than the requirements of pomp and luxury

It was not until the 20th century was drawing to a close that critics, architects and designers began questioning these stylistic precepts, asking why design had to be simple when complexity was more interesting, or why it had to be clear when ambiguity was more involving. Why not look to the past, not just the present, as inspiration for design? And what was wrong with ornament anyway? The reactionary mood led to a rebellion in design and the 1980s saw these very rigid principles of Good Design flouted by a younger generation eager to create chaos and celebrate diversity.

Many of Kaufmann's 'shoulds' have been tempered by a 21st-century appreciation of the breadth of design. 'Modern Design's' principles and goals, which had been so tightly focused, have expanded widely. Whereas Kaufmann judged objects separately in terms of form, function and economics, contemporary consumers must now judge design in a larger context that delves into the circumstances of its creation, production and marketing, its social, environmental and technological issues, as well as where the object sits within their own lives as a 'loved object'.

Whereas 'Modern Design' adhered to a single aesthetic viewpoint, today the lines are not so distinct. In an age of homogenisation, globalisation and supersaturation, there is a rallying cry against a material world in which everything has the same utilitarian touch. Both the creative spirit of the designer and the increasing sophistication of the consumer have played their roles in directing design's future – asking for individuality, emotion and subjectivity in place of objective rationing.

GOOD
DESIGN
IS
MAKING
SOMETHING
INTELLIGIBLE
AND
MEMORABLE.

GREAT
DESIGN
IS
MAKING
SOMETHING
MEMORABLE
AND
MEANINGFUL.

Good design is a renaissance attitude that combines technology, cognitive science, human need and beauty to produce something that the world didn't know it was missing.

Paola Antonelli, Senior Curator, Department of Architecture and Design, Museum of Modern Art, New York [30]

COLLECTIBLES

At the beginning of the 21st century, the proliferation of design has saturated our environment – from our bodies to our homes and workplaces, our modes of transport, and every aspect of our lives. Demarcating what is collectible – as opposed to what is simply consumed – has become as challenging as identifying what design is, while the debate over how to describe collectible design is similarly plagued by insufficient semantics. Terms such as *limited-edition design, design art, autonomous design* and *high design* fall short as a catchall phrase.

Not all the works under the collector's gaze are, or were, intentionally limited in their output: 20th-century interior designs from Marcel Breuer, Alvar Aalto, Jean Prouvé, Charlotte Perriand, Charles and Ray Eames, Giò Ponti and Poul Kjaerholm were never conceived to be produced in limited volume. They are rare because their production quotas were stunted due to the limitations of the industry and therefore never progressed past a handful of examples, or the works simply have been lost to history. Other designs – such as the early Art Deco triumphs by Eileen Gray, the exquisitely crafted works of George Nakashima and Alexandre Noll, the roguish creations of Ettore Sottsass or Ron Arad, and the raw designs of Nacho Carbonell or Peter Marigold – could only exist as unique, stand-alone works due to the hand-craftsmanship involved in their production.

The term 'design art' was coined in 1999 by Alexander Payne, worldwide director of design for auction house Phillips de Pury, to differentiate between the fine arts, the applied arts and then the design arts – i.e. functional objects produced since the industrial revolution. The auction house has subsequently dropped the 'art' and concluded that this is design, albeit one facet of it.

In 2005, the critic Alex Coles published his interpretation in his book *Design Art* through an investigation into artists working with design typologies. This spin on the term discussed works ranging from Matisse's interiors for Rockefeller's town house to the fabric designs Takashi Murakami conceived with Marc Jacobs.

In these contexts, the term had an approximation of validity, but for many the negative connotations of the term 'design art', when applied to all collectible design, suggest a reduction or displacement of design as a marginalised sector of art – that it can only be valid because of art; that it could never stand on its own.

Terms such as 'high design', 'connoisseurial design' or 'museum quality' are more accommodating, but still imply a level of sophistication that is more to do with market perception than the design itself. Often works are rough, ready, crude and specifically impermanent, but this would do little to hinder their likelihood of being eagerly sought by connoisseurs and institutions alike.

What is perceived as collectible is in the eye of the collector. Yet this perception is informed as much by the collective as the

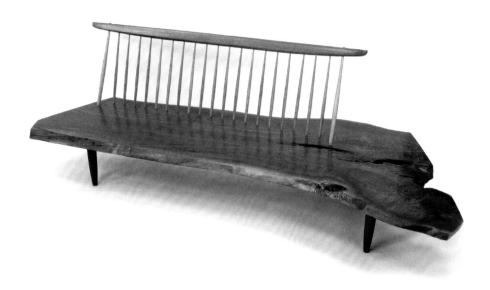

George Nakashima
Conoid bench
1966

individual. Often an entire genre or generation of work can languish for decades until with one small flick they tip to become covetable.

Ultimately, it is all design. There is no real need for hybridised terms such as 'design art' – though this particularly sought-after echelon is, as Phillips de Pury concluded, just one facet of a much larger discipline. Perhaps it is best to simply acknowledge and celebrate these specific works for their ability to embody both the tangible (exotic or luxurious materials, high-quality fabrication, documented provenances) and the intangible (excellence, expression, narrative, historical positioning and rarity).

UNIQUENESS

When designer Ron Arad founded One Off Limited in 1981, little did he realise the floodgate he was opening. Or perhaps he did. In an era in which the effects of over-consumption, over-production, globalisation, homogenisation and disposability

Ron Arad
Concrete stereo
1983

are debated daily, the desire for unique works reflects a larger
socio-cultural drive. Consumers and collectors alike seek to
surround themselves with objects that speak to their sense
of individuality. Designers, for their part, seek to imbue their
products with personality and narrative in order to add another
layer – emotional value. It is an antidote to the ubiquity of
mass-manufactured objects and a variation on the quest for
sustainability: a unique object that is cherished for its inherent
qualities is more likely to sustain the test of time.

One-off designs, however, are not simply a response to a
socio-cultural malaise or market demand, but often the only
valid option for an object and its designer. Indeed, many of the
Bauhäuslers'[31] products could not be industrially produced
until the 1990s, when technological standards finally reached

a level that allowed their apparently simple but technically highly complex forms to be manufactured in volume.

Historically, designers have viewed themselves as explorers, testing the tolerance between materials, process and medium. The journey is often of more interest and importance than the destination. Depending on the materials or process employed, some objects could never be replicated. From Arts and Crafts to Art Deco and even Modernism, there exist many examples of works that were either intentionally or inadvertently left as a one-off. As the designer Tom Dixon has said, 'from a historical view, if you go all the way back to the Arts and Crafts movement, there's nothing really new in making smaller batches of things which are unique and new and for a more rarefied market. There will always be people working outside the system because either they are ahead of the curve and innovative or because it's not fashionable or too peculiar to sell. It's always happened, but I think what is new is that people are starting to understand that it could be collectible, that it could have a have value beyond just the pure design element.'[32]

The constraints of the industry (cost, efficiency, mass appeal) are now so rigid that they can limit the creative possibilities of design.

When design isn't dependent on industry, it can express opinions. Designers can use this questioning – of the relationship of the object to its use and to its end user – to shape their work. They can also use the industrial model to question (or even challenge) the production system, its social role and responsibility in producing objects.

At a time when the Modernist dream of standardisation has expired, designers have used technology to embed unique characteristics into manufactured objects. Dutch designer Hella Jongerius has been a leading proponent of this approach; she has brought a humanising element to her industrial designs, such as in her 'B-Set' bowls for Royal Tichelaar Makkum, which contain intentional flaws created during the firing process.

Hella Jongerius
B-Set bowls
1988

---

*Because money is so important in the industry, manufacturers
don't have time, they don't want to wait, so they want the product
to be in the market straight away. In order for the product to be in
the market straight away, the designer does not have a chance to
try to design a new product. As you know, when you are designing
a new product your eye has to be familiar with that product so it
can sell straight away. No company wants to wait two or three
years to think it is going to sell. The market constraints for the
designers are so great – in fact, they cannot create.*

Didier Krzentowski, director, Galerie Kreo, Paris[33]

*When I started off [in the 1980s], I wasn't thinking of my work
as limited edition. It was limited by the fact that it was made with
found objects, so it was impossible to make the same piece twice.
I was limited by circumstance, really.*

Tom Dixon, designer, London[34]

These artefacts are hugely important to society and to the world. They are valuable, they have changed the world, whether that be a Marc Newson design, a Picasso drawing, a Le Corbusier building or Einstein's E=mc² sketch. You feel the importance of them through their very presence. That is the thing I like, and I think that is why people desire to own a one-off, because there is none other anywhere else.

Tony Chambers, editor-in-chief, *Wallpaper**[35]

PROTOTYPE

As the name suggests, the prototype is the first draft of an object – an industrial template – that holds the DNA of a design idea. It is the phase between the initial concept and the fully formed object in production. Although some prototypes are simply maquettes, rough models or process examples in order to test structure, form or material, increasingly sophisticated production processes mean that some prototypes could be considered an absolute object in their own right.

The objects might be characterised by a technical or material discrepancy, compared to the final product, but they can hold a rare charm; there is an increased closeness to the designer's imagination, and a directness to the making that often changes when manufacturing and marketing forces are fully integrated.

Alongside their role as a launchpad for an idea, prototypes are often used to attract media and industrial attention. While many prototypes remain at sketch stage, those that are developed into serial production pieces or an editioned series become highly prized by designer, manufacturer, gallerist or dealer and collector alike. The idea of owning the prototype of a mass-manufactured object – the imperfect genesis of a totally perfect and successful idea – is a seductive and rewarding option.

A prototype is a step in the design process. It can stop there, but, if it does, it means that it has failed. In order to be successful, a prototype has to be followed by industrial development or multiple editions.

Pierre Keller, director, ÉCAL, Lausanne[35]

However, the description of some objects as a prototype is circumspect, for often what is presented as a prototype is simply a way of increasing an edition size. As James Zemaitis, director of 20th-century design at Sotheby's, has said: 'There's two versions of the prototype. There's the prototype as something that Isamu Noguchi made in 1952 that was an absolute bomb, and he couldn't get it right and he puts it away until he actually figures out how to do it. And the prototype is like A and everything else is like B. Then there's the limited-edition market where many people ask, "When is enough enough here?" You've got an edition of 20 plus three artist proofs plus five prototypes. Well, okay so that's actually 28. Is there any difference between one and 28 besides the price tag? And the answer varies.'[37]

LIMITED EDITION

In art, the term edition originally referred to a finite series of impressions taken from the work – be it a fine-art print, a photograph or sculpture. In order to control this series the editions are usually limited to a set number, be that two or 2,000, and authenticated by the artist and date of production. Given design's conventional propensity to be made in editions, many galleries and designers have employed the art-world model to create and control a limited edition of certain designs. Galleries such as Galerie Kreo in Paris, founded by Didier and Clémence Krzentowski in 1999, follow this principle, often with an edition of eight pieces, with two artist's proofs and two that are not for sale. As avid art and design collectors, it was a system that felt familiar to the Krzentowskis, but also one that inevitably makes the object more desirable, as a limited number of collectors will have the opportunity of owning the object.

The price of an editioned design work often increases as the edition gets closer to completion. The buyer of number 90 in a limited edition of 100 is likely to pay more than the buyer of number 12. The important thing for a collector to be aware of is how many items there are in the edition, and to have some form of documentation from the gallery or dealer stating which number of the edition has been purchased.

It's a question of market forces. After the whole explosion of interest in French 1940s furniture that started about a decade ago, dealers began to cultivate contemporary designers and place them in a high art context, aping the language of the art world – 'limited edition', 'signed and numbered' – to make collectors understand that the value of these things is not necessarily tied to the idea of what a chair should be worth or what a chair does; to approach the idea more from the point of view of art as singular creations, one-of-a-kinds, whose merit and worth were invested in the concept of the piece, the execution of the piece, divorced from questions of function.

Mayer Rus, design editor, *LA Times*[38]

Limited edition gives you the opportunity to do something that otherwise you'd never have the chance to do. But you also have responsibilities: towards yourself and where you stand, for instance. As a studio, we do limited editions and spend a lot of money on them ... We do these things because it makes it possible to develop an academic way of working within a studio.

Jurgen Bey, designer, Rotterdam[39]

Throughout history, some designs have been necessarily limited in their production, often due to the manufacturing context, or the cost or availability of the chosen materials. Such pieces are also notable for their quality, through the use of a particular technique or a high level of craftsmanship.

In 2007 the London/New York antiques house Mallet advocated a variation on the crafts renaissance. The pre-eminent 18th-century-furniture specialist took the unprecedented step of moving into the 21st century with the launch of Meta – a range of objects that merged contemporary design with peerless craftsmanship, with the aim of celebrating and securing the future of endangered skills. By their very nature, the objects had to be limited in their production. For his 'Fig-Leaf' wardrobe in this range, Tord Boontje took 18 months to develop and incorporate 616 hand-enamelled fig leaves – each of which took up to six hours to paint – made by some of the last remaining enamellers in the English Midlands. The substructure holding

Tord Boontje
Fig-Leaf wardrobe
2008

the leaves was made in Angers in western France; the internal tree was sculpted then cast by Patrick Blanchard in Paris; the silk background was woven by the Gainsborough Silk Weaving Company in Suffolk; and all the various components were brought together in Cambridge. Given the extreme labour-intensity, and the concomitantly high prices that such a work commands, Meta predicted that it could only achieve three wardrobes per year.

WHAT

Producing limited editions is also commercial opportunism by both designers and manufacturers. There are only a handful of sophisticated manufacturers who will make large-scale investments in individual designers, working with them on a complex level over long periods of time with crack engineers and amazing materials, developing specialist tools or machinery to create equally special processes. Naturally, these are the companies that every product designer or furniture designer longs to work for, but obviously they only employ a handful, and those designers are only chosen because they have somehow come to the manufacturer's attention. The easiest way for a designer to achieve this is by designing and making their own work.

The same applies to manufacturers. As Alice Rawsthorn, design critic for the *International Herald Tribune*, acknowledges, 'Vitra had always refused to produce limited editions, and then it did a series of anniversary editions. It could be read as Vitra's acceptance that if it wanted a little media coverage, this was what it had to do.'[40]

Alongside this is a generational change: a new era of designers, having watched their predecessors produce stand-alone works in the 1980s and 1990s, no longer aspire to work industrially, and instead opt for one-off or editioned batches. The polarising debate between Modernism and Postmodernism had been played out, and the new generation was born into a design world that accepted complexity and diversity as standards.

The concept of a limited edition has been, however, debased and devalued through overuse and abuse. Just as consumers were bombarded with 'designer furniture', now they are presented with 'limited-edition' consumer items on every supermarket shelf. From fast food to cars, limited edition has been misaligned with the phrase 'for a limited time only' in marketing campaigns, reducing the goods to just that – a marketing conceit, Design's adoption of the term has produced similar negative consequences.

The idea of making eight copies of a gold-plated version of an existing object to sell directly at auction was widespread; there were was a demand to meet this supply with wealthy individuals prepared to pay premium prices. (In the art world, Damien Hirst is probably the most successful example of such a strategy – an industry, even – of limited editions.) Such practices can, however, superficially inflate prices beyond their true value and open works to criticism from the media, industry and collector alike.

The question is always asked, 'How long can this go on for?'
Well, for quite a while if the people involved are respectful ... If
it's not handled properly, the ultimate losers can be the designers
themselves, with the value of their own work crashing. Pieces
can be put into the market that don't really warrant being there,
or there can be no reason for them to be an edition or a one-off.
It's our responsibility to ensure that the pieces we're promoting
are pieces that we believe in, with a valid reason for their price.
Otherwise, the bubble could very well burst on this industry.

Alasdhair Willis, director, Established & Sons, London[41]

Something on my list for years was 'You Can't Lay Down Your
Memory' chest of drawers by Tejo Remy, a key piece from the
early 1990s. But we only bought one at the V&A in 2008.
Beforehand we had long debated which one from the series we
should get. As it's an edition of 200, we could have just bought
the latest off the line. But it didn't feel like the right thing to do.
Eventually we found number 22 ... about as early as we
reckoned we were going to get.

Gareth Williams, Senior Tutor of Design Products at
the Royal College of Art, formerly Curator of 20th-century
and contemporary furniture at the V&A, London[42]

ARTIST PROOFS

As in the art world, many designers make proof copies of their
work, the number of which can vary. Normally these proofs are
somewhere between the prototype and the finished object,
but sometimes they are almost identical to the finished work.
Artist's proofs (or APs) exist to provide some sort of insurance
for the designer in the event that the work increases in value
– giving the designer an opportunity to either keep hold of or
independently sell the work in the future. However, it is an ill-
defined system, as the number or proofs, their determined value
or hierarchy in the edition and who actually keeps hold of them
(gallery or designer) is determined by the gallery and designer
with each new edition. As with all purchases, the collector
should receive documentation confirming the object's lineage
(AP, Prototype, Edition or Unique).

WHAT

REISSUED DESIGN

With the rise of design manufacturing came the need for marketable content to manufacture. Savvy manufacturers have sought the licence to put key examples of existent designs back into production and reissue them to a wider audience. Companies continue to manufacture the works that they produced while the designers were still alive, but there are subtle (and some not-so-subtle) differences between the works manufactured during a designer's lifetime and the more recent iterations of their work. There is obviously a marked difference of value between owning an original (or one close to the original design date, in the case of manufactured work) and owning a later example of the same work.

The special case about [Poul] Kjaerholm is that during his lifetime the essence of his career was mass-production. His masterworks were mass-produced. He had a very significant first edition run through Kold Christensen, a company that he helped found. Then, the rights to that furniture were taken on into a second edition by another company, Fritz Hansen. Collectors who come to auction and secondary market dealers are looking for the first-edition Kold Christensen pieces, not the second editions that you can still pick up today. But then, of course, there's the whole idea of reissuing new pieces that were not in production for all of these years. Going back to the workshop period of Poul Kjaerholm when he was very, very young, and taking prototypes that he did in the late 1940s and early 1950s and reissuing them in limited editions now? I think that's a cause of significant controversy in terms of market value and secondary market value. Buying a reissue of a 1952 chair in a limited edition of 10 – are you buying that because you love it? Are you buying that because you're hoping to flip it 10 years from now? It's a contentious issue, to say the least!

James Zemaitis, director of 20th-century design,
Sotheby's, New York[43]

56

Limited editions are not worth less if a company is also producing mass-market versions of them, because they are two different objects. They may look similar, but one's made out of different materials and in a different way. The existence of both is usually a positive thing, as it enhances the piece's ability to be recognised. What is really important is that as a gallery, you don't confuse the two. If the designer goes down both roads, you keep yourself on one side or the other.

Barry Friedman, Friedman Benda Gallery, New York[44]

Poul Kjaerholm
Lounge chair, model no. PKO,
designed 1952, executed 1997

MANUFACTURED VERSUS UNIQUE

MAARTEN BAAS, 'SMOKE'

For most designers, the democratisation of design is the ultimate paradigm. To have their drawings, sketches and ideas realised as commercial objects, produced in volume by international manufacturers before being disseminated to a wider audience, is the ultimate validation of their work. But with design accounting for 6.2% of all graduates in the UK alone,[45] catching the attention of manufacturers is increasingly hard for even the experienced designer. Indeed, neophyte manufacturers seeking fresh talent often do so to the exclusion of more established designers.

The characteristics that make an object suitable for commercial manufacture are diverse, and the industry's requirements rigorous. Considerations of suitability, costs of preparing the tooling as well as the costs of the actual production, marketability and distribution: all determine an object's manufacturability. Once through this obstacle course, the industrial process can often introduce small changes that destroy the spirit of the original design, and uniqueness is forfeited by repetition on a large scale. Nevertheless, designers still persevere. Designing for industry and creating unique works are, however, not mutually exclusive. Prototypes can be experimental steps towards manufacture, while the lessons learned from industrial practice can inform a designer's knowledge of the market, materials and process, ultimately informing their studio practice.

In contemporary design, rarely does a single body of work receive both gallery and industry attention, with the one designer satisfying the two very different needs simultaneously. Rarely do emerging designers secure industrial support straight out of college either – rarely, but not never. On presentation of his 2002 Design Academy Eindhoven graduate collection at the International Furniture Fair in Milan, Maarten Baas proved the exception to those rules. His work, the charred remains of some long-forgotten furniture pieces, was the star attraction of that year's fair and received the praise and attention of all who saw it.

Through the 'Smoke' range, Baas subverted convention. For a trade fair that is predicated on the new, he chose to present the un-new. 'Smoke' could be perceived as a sly but worthy comment on the industry; however, the nuances behind it are much richer. Designed in a period in which the world itself was on fire – post-September 11; wars raging in the Middle East; natural disasters escalating – 'Smoke' felt like the apotheosis of its time: dark, violent and full of unanswered questions.

The process Baas used to create the 'Smoke' series was paradoxically straightforward: he took existing objects, scorched them with a blowtorch, then impregnated and sealed the charred remains with an epoxy resin to render them useful again.

Lina Kanafani of London-based design store Mint was one of the first to approach Baas about his degree collection, but it was the Dutch manufacturing firm Moooi (recently founded by Casper Vissers and designer Marcel Wanders) that was the first to apply for rights to manufacture the work. It was a highly unlikely choice for a young company. Not only did the overtly conceptual series demand unpredictable and labour-intensive processes, but as Vissers explains, 'In those days Maarten was not the hero he is today [Baas was Design Miami/'s Designer of the Year for 2009]. But also, Moooi was very young too, we were in the first years of the company... when Marcel presented these to me, I thought, Wow! It's a nice PR piece but we will never sell one. But the opposite happened. It became what we call an "evergreen", whereby if a product can sell for three years at high speeds, it probably will continue selling after 10 years.'[46]

I have a particular affinity to his use of originally insignificant and ugly pieces in his 'Smoke' series. I simply love that whole transformative process, which then saves those pieces from probable oblivion. Similarly, I am not particularly interested in 'smoking' the Classics, as for me they already have a considerable and valuable life of their own, which means they are in no need of being rewritten or rescued.

Lina Kanafani, Mint, London[47]

I didn't intend for it to be a mass-produced product because it doesn't scream 'mass-production', but Moooi were willing to try. You have to have a producer who is willing to experiment.

Maarten Baas, designer, Den Bosch[48]

Maarten Baas
Smoke armchair
2002 (issued 2004)

Very little was changed to translate Baas's graduation pieces into the mass-manufactured chandelier, armchair and dining chair. Instead of using found furniture, though, Moooi employed craftspeople in the Philippines to first make copies of the ornate originals and then to burn and preserve them to the same formula. The results are a beguiling facsimile; even the charring seems identical from one object to the next. A curious characteristic of Baas's original chandelier was that one of its wooden arms had been burned to a charred stump: the Moooi pieces faithfully reproduce this. 'I can't tell you how it happens,' Baas admits, 'maybe they even don't make that arm at all.'[42]

Vissers champions the veracity with which the company handles the work. 'Even Philippe Starck asked us to do a range of "Smoke" with colour. But we were adamant; we will never do colours, even if we can sell thousands or hundreds of thousands.

Its not true to Maarten's prototype concept.'[50] However, he is also realistic about the limitations of serial production; aware that the Moooi strand of the story ends after the first chapter. Baas concurs: 'the Moooi works are a moment in time and the value of that moment is being mass-produced. I obviously enjoy working with them, but the mass products will never have the story – they are anonymous pieces, and the story remains within the prototype.'[51]

Maarten Baas
Smoke chandelier
2002 (issued 2004)

If the purpose of 'Smoke' is to celebrate the prototype and the composite thoughts inherent in that first model, then the narrative continues through Baas's dialogue with Murray Moss, founder of the influential design store Moss in New York. Moss had also seen the 2002 Eindhoven presentation and, although indifferent to the choice of furniture Baas had burned, was compelled by the intrinsic and emotional qualities of the series. He interpreted

'Smoke' not as a process of destruction, nor as a celebration of a particular finish, but as a visible representation of the lessons Baas had ingested as a student of design: 'a comment, a re-working of that education ... It's like a snake eating an elephant; you recognise the elephant, it's part of the snake, and yet you still see the elephant.'[52]

The physical act of 'spewing out' this design history was the motivation for Moss's 2004 *Where There's Smoke ...* exhibition, for which Baas burnt some of the most iconic examples of various aesthetic movements, including Jugendstil, mid-20th century and contemporary design.

Gerrit Rietveld
Red-and-blue chair
1918–23

The press release for the exhibition states, 'As in the great steam engines of the 19th century, Baas proposes design as a "fuel" which, when thrown on the fire, releases energy to propel us forward ... Their authorship and identity altered, they become revisionist, highly personal, audacious expressions of Baas, all now related through his personal experience and through the eloquence of their metamorphosis.'

By inviting Baas to ingest and disgorge Gerrit Rietveld and Marc Newson (among many others), Moss converted Baas's burning of existent furniture types into a performance – 'an encounter between Baas and Frank Lloyd Wright. A souvenir of an encounter, and that's why that's to me a valuable object, because those personal encounters are rare.'[53]

Maarten Baas
Where There's Smoke /Red-and-blue
chair (Rietveld), 2004

Gerrit Rietveld
Zig Zag chair
1939

As Moss stresses, however, it is a personal encounter with the designer, which is not something always available or desirable to the collector. Regardless, it is important when considering a collection of design to understand the differences between manufactured works and editioned works, even if they seem to come from the same place.

Spontaneity is missing in so many rationalised products that go from a sketch, to a computer rendering, to a prototype and at the end, there is no heart and soul any more.

Penny Sparke, design historian, London [54]

If someone asked me to burn an Ikea chair, then I wouldn't be interested, but if that chair went to the director of Ikea because he is starting to feel different about his own product, then that would become interesting. It's not only the product; it's the story around the product that gives it value.

Maarten Baas, designer, Den Bosch [55]

Maarten Baas
Where There's Smoke/Zig Zag chair
(Rietveld), 2002

CASE STUDY

Ettore Sottsass
Carlton divider shelf
1981

Maarten Baas
Where There's Smoke/Carlton divider
shelf (Sottsass), 2004

CASE STUDY

DESIGN
SINCE THE 1830S

1

2

3

1837

1837
ROYAL COLLEGE OF ART, London

1850

1851
GREAT EXHIBITION, London

VICTORIA AND ALBERT MUSEUM OPENS
London, 1857

1

A.W.N. PUGIN
Early Victorian oak three-leafed screen (1850)

With over 150 years of design history, this timeline is by no means an exhaustive or comprehensive list. However, it does cover the launch of major or influential movements in design and architecture, the launch of important and iconic design works, the debut of influential or canonical exhibitions, the development of key materials and the launch publication dates of informative magazines. Works illustrated are numbered where they appear in the timeline, and are dated where they appear unless otherwise stated.

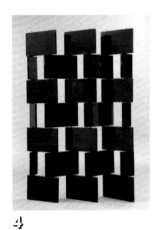

4

5

6

1860

1867
KARL MARX publishes *Das Kapital*
(*Capital: A Critique of Political Economy*)

1880

1880s
ART NOUVEAU AND
ARTS & CRAFTS MOVEMENTS

2
CHARLES RENNIE MACKINTOSH
Ladderback chairs (c. 1903)

7

8

9

1890

1896
THE ARCHITECTURAL REVIEW, London
LOUIS SULLIVAN coins the maxim 'form ever follows function'

1897
VIENNA SECESSION
ART ET DÉCORATION is published Librairie centrale des Beaux-Arts, Paris, edited by François Thiébault-Sisson

1900

1903
WIENER WERKSTÄTTE
Founded by Josef Hoffmann and Koloman Moser, Vienna
FORD MOTOR COMPANY, Detroit, Michigan

1904
GEORG JENSEN WORKSHOP, Copenhagen

1905
SIGMUND FREUD publishes *Three Essays of the Theory of Sexuality*

1907
PICASSO AND CUBISM
DEUTSCHE WERKBUND founded by Hermann Muthesius, Munich
BAKELITE, the world's first synthetic plastic, patented by Belgian chemist Dr Leo Baekeland
ADOLF LOOS publishes *Ornament and Crime*

1908
MODEL-T FORD
OLIVETTI COMPANY, Turin
IDEAL HOME EXHIBITION, London

1909
MARINETTI'S FUTURIST MANIFESTO
published in *Le Figaro*, Paris

10

11

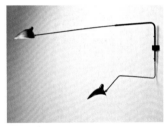

12

1910

1913
FORMICA PATENTED,
Cincinnati, Ohio

1914
OUTBREAK OF WW1

1915
DESIGN AND INDUSTRIES ASSOCIATION,
forerunner of Design Council, UK

KASIMIR MALEVICH LAUNCHES SUPREMATISM,
Petrograd (now Saint Petersburg)

1916
DADAIST MOVEMENT, Zurich

1917
DE STIJL MOVEMENT, THE NETHERLANDS,
founded by artists, designers and architects including
Theo van Doesburg and Piet Mondrian

CONSTRUCTIVISM, Soviet Union

3
GERRIT RIETVELD
Red-and-blue chair (c.1918)

1918
LA RINASCENTE, department store, Milan

MATSUSHITA ELECTRIC INDUSTRIAL
COMPANY, Osaka

1919
BAUHAUS SCHOOL founded by Walter Gropius,
Weimar, Germany

TREATY OF VERSAILLES

LLOYD LOOM PATENT ADVERTISED

1920

1920s
ART DECO MOVEMENT

4
EILEEN GRAY
Screen (1922)

MODERNIST MOVEMENT, France

1921
BRAUN COMPANY, Frankfurt-am-Main, Germany

ALESSI COMPANY, Omegna, Italy

1923
HERMAN MILLER FURNITURE COMPANY,
Zeeland, Michigan

LE CORBUSIER publishes *Vers
une Architecture*

FIRST TRIENNALE, Monza, Italy

1925
BAUHAUS SCHOOL MOVES TO DESSAU,
Germany

5
MARCEL BREUER
Club chair B3 (Wassily)

EXPOSITION DES ARTS DÉCORATIFS
ET INDUSTRIELS, Paris

6
EMILE-JACQUES RULHMANN
Cabonel Chiffonier (1921–2)

CRANBROOK ACADEMY OF ART,
Bloomfield Hills, Michigan

1926
NOVOCENTO MOVEMENT, Italy

CONTAINER CORPORATION
manufactures first cardboard packaging,
St Louis, Missouri

1927
CASSINA COMPANY, Milan

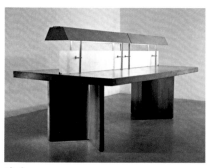

13   **14**   **15**

1928
DOMUS MAGAZINE founded by Giò Ponti, Milan
INTERNATIONAL CONGRESS OF MODERN
ARCHITECTS (CIAM) organized by Le Corbusier,
at Chateau de la Sarraz, Switzerland
BUCKMINSTER FULLER'S
'DYMAXION' CONCEPT

1929
MUSEUM OF MODERN ART (MOMA),
New York, opens
WALL STREET STOCK MARKET CRASH
EXPOSICIÓN INTERNACIONAL DE BARCELONA

7
LUDWIG MIES VAN DER ROHE
Barcelona model MR 90 chair

1930

1930
MILAN TRIENNALE
ART CENTER COLLEGE OF DESIGN,
Pasadena, California
GUNNAR ASPLUND AND BRUNO MATHSSON,
design for Stockholm exhibition promoting
Swedish Modernism

1931
EMPIRE STATE BUILDING COMPLETED, New York
ISOKON BY WELLS COATES WITH JACK AND
MOLLY PRITCHARD, London
LE CORBUSIER'S VILLA SAVOYE COMPLETED,
Poissy, France

1932
THE INTERNATIONAL STYLE
ARCHITECTURE SINCE 1922 exhibition,
MoMA, New York

1933
BAUHAUS OFFICIALLY CLOSES
CHICAGO'S CENTURY OF PROGRESS FAIR draws
10 million admissions in its first season
BLACK MOUNTAIN COLLEGE, Asheville,
North Carolina
RAYMOND LOEWY designs S-I steam locomotive
for Pennsylvania Railroad

8
JEAN ROYÉRE
Armchair (c. 1936)

1935
FRANK LLOYD WRIGHT builds his masterpiece,
Fallingwater, Allegheny Mountains, Pennsylvania
PLEXIGLAS (PERSPEX) PATENTED,
Esslingen, Germany
ARTEK COMPANY founded by Alvar Aalto,
Helsinki, Finland

9
ALVAR AALTO
Paimio chair (1930)

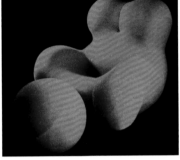

16   17   18

1936
NIKOLAUS PEVSNER publishes *Pioneers of the Modern Movement*

SPANISH CIVIL WAR

1937
BAUHAUS PROFESSORS Ludwig Mies van der Rohe, Herbert Bayer, Walter Gropius, László Maholy-Nagy and Marcel Breuer emigrate to the US

EXPOSITION UNIVERSELLE, Paris

1938
FIBREGLASS patented by Russell Games Slayter for Owens-Corning, Toledo, Ohio

KNOLL INTERNATIONAL FURNITURE COMPANY, New York

1939
WORLD OF TOMORROW, World's Fair, New York

HITLER INVADES POLAND
OUTBREAK OF WWII

1940

1941
UTILITY MOVEMENT, UK

1942
THE AMERICAN CRAFTSMEN'S COUNCIL, New York

ORGANIC DESIGN IN HOME FURNISHINGS exhibition, MoMA, New York

1943
IKEA COMPANY, Älmhult, Sweden

1944
COUNCIL OF INDUSTRIAL DESIGN (later the Design Council), London

1945
WWII ENDS

1946
FIRST GENERAL PURPOSE COMPUTER, the 'ENIAC', built, Philadelphia

NEW FURNITURE DESIGNED BY CHARLES EAMES exhibition, MoMA, New York

DU PONT'S TUPPERWARE INTRODUCED, Orlando, Florida

BRITAIN CAN MAKE IT exhibition, Victoria and Albert Museum, London

ARTELUCE COMPANY, Milan

CAPPELLINI COMPANY, Milan

1947
ACADEMY FOR INDUSTRIAL DESIGN EINDHOVEN (today the Design Academy Eindhoven), The Netherlands

CHRISTIAN DIOR'S NEW LOOK, Paris

1948
SIGFRIED GIEDION publishes *Mechanisation Takes Command*

1949
PHILIP JOHNSON'S GLASS HOUSE, New Canaan, Connecticut

KARTELL COMPANY, Milan

BUCKMINSTER FULLER'S GEODESIC DOME

COLOGNE FURNITURE FAIR (Internationale Möbelmesse, IMM)

19   20   21

1950

1950
VITRA COMPANY, Weil am Rhein, Germany
COMPUTER-AIDED DESIGN (CAD) originated
at the Massachusetts Institute of Technology, Cambridge

10
HANS WEGNER
Dolphin chair

11
ALEXANDRE NOLL
Dining table

1951
FESTIVAL OF BRITAIN, London
ASPEN INTERNATIONAL DESIGN CONFERENCES,
Colorado

1952
FIRST HYDROGEN BOMB TESTED BY THE US

1954
ZANOTTA COMPANY, Italy

12
SERGE MOUILLE
Two-arm wall light

1955
WARSAW PACT
OTL AICHER co-founds Hochschule für Gestaltung,
Ulm, Germany

1956
THIS IS TOMORROW exhibition, Whitechapel Gallery,
London
SOLOMON R. GUGGENHEIM MUSEUM OPENS,
New York
ALISON + PETER SMITHSON'S
THE HOUSE OF THE FUTURE, *Daily Mail* Ideal Home
Show, London
MUSEUM OF CONTEMPORARY CRAFTS OPENS,
New York

13
GIÒ PONTI
Superleggera side chair

1957
14
ACHILLE AND PIER GIACOMO CASTIGLIONI
Mezzadro stool

1958
CARBON FIBRE patented by Dr Roger Bacon,
Cleveland, Ohio

1959
NORTH VIETNAM DECLARES WAR
ON SOUTH VIETNAM

22   **23**   **24**

1960

1960
REYNER BANHAM publishes *Theory and Design in the First Machine Age*
ANTI-DESIGN/RADICAL DESIGN MOVEMENT, Italy

1961
BERLIN WALL ERECTED
SOVIETS LAUNCH FIRST MAN INTO SPACE
SALONE DEL MOBILE (Milan Furniture Fair), with only Italian exhibitors
EERO SAARINEN'S TWA TERMINAL BUILDING, Idlewild Airport, New York

1962
DIETER RAMS appointed Director of Braun
CENTRUM INDUSTRIËLE VORMGEVING, Amsterdam

1963
ARCHIGRAM FOUNDED, London
INGO MAURER'S DESIGN M, Munich

1964
HABITAT STORE, London
KEN ADAM DESIGNS SETS for the films *Dr Strangelove* and *Goldfinger*

1965
BULLET TRAIN, Japan
MAO ZEDONG'S CULTURAL REVOLUTION
KILKENNY DESIGN WORKSHOPS, Ireland

1966
ROBERT VENTURI publishes *Complexity and Contradiction in Modern Architecture*
SUPERSTUDIO AND ARCHIZOOM, Florence

15
PIERRE JEANNERET
Illuminated library table

16
SUPERSTUDIO
Bazaar seating environment (1968)

FANTASY FURNITURE exhibition, Museum of Contemporary Crafts, New York

1967
2001: A SPACE ODYSSEY, Stanley Kubrick's film, features Olivier Mourgue's Djin series furniture
SALONE DEL MOBILE allows international exhibitors for first time

1969
AMERICAN ASTRONAUTS LAND ON THE MOON
ARPANET DEFENSE SYSTEM (precursor to Internet) developed by the US government
CENTRE DE CRÉATION INDUSTRIELLE, Paris

17
GAETANO PESCE
Donna Up5 chair

25

26

27

1970

1970
AMERICAN CRAFT MOVEMENT

18
WENDELL CASTLE
Crescent Rocker (1982)

1971
VICTOR PAPANEK publishes *Design for the Real World: Human Ecology and Social Change*

19
GINO SARFATTI
Floor lamp

1972
ITALY: THE NEW DOMESTIC LANDSCAPE exhibition, MoMA, New York

20
JOE COLOMBO
Tube chair (1969–70)

1973
GLOBAL OIL CRISIS

1974
B&B ITALIA COMPANY, Italy
FIAC (CONTEMPORARY ART FAIR), Paris

1975
TEFAF MAASTRICHT/PICTURA FINE ART FAIR

1976
APPLE COMPUTER FOUNDED, California

1977
CENTRE GEORGES POMPIDOU OPENS, Paris
CHARLES JENCKS publishes *The Language of Post-Modern Architecture*
MODO MAGAZINE edited by Alessandro Mendini, Milan

1980

1980
RAPID PROTOTYING
i-D AND *THE FACE* MAGAZINES, London

1981
MEMPHIS GROUP, Milan

21
ETTORE SOTTSASS
Biedermeier sofa (1982)

22
RON ARAD
Big Easy chair

IBM, launches first affordable personal computer
COLUMBIA, the first space shuttle, launches

1982
V&A'S *BOILERHOUSE PROJECT*,
precursor to the Design Museum, London
PHILIPPE STARCK completes private apartments for the President of France, Paris

1983
BLUEPRINT MAGAZINE, London
SWATCH COMPANY, Zürich
ALESSI OFFICINA launches tea and coffee sets by designers including Mendini and Michael Graves
RON ARAD'S ONE-OFF STUDIO, London

1985
23
GAROUSTE AND BONETTI
Prince Imperial chair

1986
FOSTER AND PARTNER'S HONG KONG AND SHANGAI BANK HEADQUARTERS, Hong Kong

24
SHIRO KURAMATA
How High the Moon chair

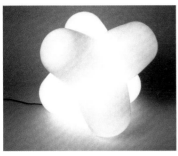

28

29

30

1987
ANDY WARHOL DIES
BLACK MONDAY CRASH IN STOCK MARKETS

1988
ISDN CONNECTIONS SPEED UP
COMMUNICATIONS
DECONSTRUCTIVIST ARCHITECTURE
exhibition, MoMA, New York
JASPER MORRISON, *Some New Items for the Home,
Part 1* exhibition, Berlin Design Wekstadt

25
JASPER MORRISON
Ply chair and Ply table

1989
INTERNATIONAL CONTEMPORARY
FURNITURE FAIR, New York
DESIGN MUSEUM, London
VITRA DESIGN MUSEUM, Weil am Rhein, Germany
TIM BERNERS-LEE INVENTS THE WORLD
WIDE WEB
BERLIN WALL FALLS
ELLE DECORATION MAGAZINE, London

1990

1990
26
PHILIPPE STARCK
Juicy Salif citrus-squeezer for Alessi

1991
FIRST STAND-ALONE DESIGN AUCTION
HELD AT BONHAMS, London

1992
LOS ANGELES MODERN AUCTIONS
first sale realises $94,000
YOUNG BRITISH ARTISTS AT SAATCHI
GALLERY, London

1993
GIJS BAKKER & RENNY RAMAKERS LAUNCH
DROOG DESIGN, Amsterdam

27
TEJO REMY
You Can't Lay Down Your Memory chest of drawers

1994
HERMAN MILLER reissues designs by Charles and
Ray Eames
100% DESIGN LONDON

1995
MAISON & OBJET, Paris
WINDOWS 95, EBAY, AMAZON
DESIGN INDABA, South Africa

1996
*WALLPAPER** MAGAZINE, London
DUTCH DESIGN CAFÉ HIGHLIGHTING WORKS
OF CONTEMPORARY DUTCH DESIGN
MoMA, New York

28
TOM DIXON
Jack light (1997)

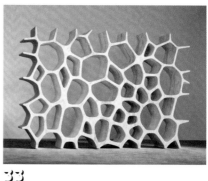

31   **32**   **33**

1997
LE PAVILLON DES ARTS ET DU DESIGN, Paris
THE INTERNATIONAL EXPOSITIONS OF
SCULPTURE OBJECTS & FUNCTIONAL ART,
New York
SENSATION exhibition, The Royal Academy of Arts,
London

1998
GOOGLE, APPLE IMAC
DESIGNERS BLOCK, London

1999
CARLO MOLLINO ASH AND BRASS ARMCHAIR
OF 1952 SELLS AT CHRISTIES FOR $129,000
CHRISTIE'S EAST REALISES $1.8M OVER 135
LOTS, New York

2000

2000
WRIGHT AUCTION HOUSE, Chicago
TATE MODERN, THE MILLENNIUM DOME,
THE LONDON EYE

2001
APPLE IPOD

2002
29
FERNANDO AND HUMBERTO CAMPANA
Banquet chair

2003
SOTHEBY'S REALISES $19.5M IN DECEMBER
DESIGN SALES, New York
ICON MAGAZINE, London
LONDON DESIGN FESTIVAL

2004
30
ATELIER VAN LIESHOUT
Prick floor lamp

2005
CARLO MOLLINO OAK AND GLASS TABLE OF
1949 SELLS AT CHRISTIE'S FOR $3.8 MILLION,
New York
LOS ANGELES MODERN AUCTIONS'
DECEMBER SALE REALISES $1.5MILLION
DESIGN MIAMI/ AND DESIGN MIAMI/BASEL
100% DESIGN TOKYO

31
ZAHA HADID
Aqua table

2006
SALONE INTERNAZIONALE DEL MOBILE
moves to new fairgrounds designed by Massimiliano
Fuksas, Milan

34

35

36

32
STUDIO JOB
Robber Baron jewel safe

2007
DESIGN ART LONDON,
later Pavilion of Art and Design, London
MARC NEWSON exhibition,
Gagosian Gallery, New York

33
MARC NEWSON
Voronoi shelf

2008
DESIGN AND THE ELASTIC MIND exhibition,
MoMA, New York
MUSEUM OF ART AND DESIGN, formerly American
Craft Museum, moves to Columbus Circle, New York
LEHMANN BROTHERS COLLAPSES

34
MARTINO GAMPER
Total Trattoria

35
KONSTANTIN GRCIC
Karbon Chaise

2009
*TELLING TALES: FEAR AND FANTASY IN
CONTEMPORARY DESIGN* exhibition,
Victoria and Albert Museum, London

36
FREDRIKSON STALLARD
Gasoline garden vase: Cadillac

2010
DESIGN MUSEUM HOLON, Israel,
designed by Ron Arad

.

CONTEMPORARY THEMES

AS
COLLECTORS'
TASTE BECOMES
MORE SOPHISTICATED
THEY WILL NATURALLY GRAVITATE
TO THE INTELLECTUALLY ENGAGED
DESIGNERS WHO CURRENTLY
DON'T REALLY HAVE
MUCH OF A
MARKET
VALUE
BUT
ARE
PRODUCING
INTERESTING
WORK, THEIRS IS
THE WORK THAT IS BEING
COLLECTED BY INSTITUTIONS AND
WILL BE INCREASINGLY COLLECTED
BY INDIVIDUALS IN THE FUTURE.

An understanding of the various themes in contemporary design and the motivations behind them are key to navigating the bewildering landscape of objects being produced and collected today. It is no longer possible simply to categorise design by type, or to make generalisations about time-specific 'isms', as everything is happening concurrently. We have no real need for another chair, yet the motivation for designing or desiring another chair does not cease. Design and desire respond to too many subjective needs for them to stop because of functional demand. Even in the face of global problems caused by over-production, pollution and energy consumption, design can hold its head high while trying to find solutions to these problems.

Contemporary design is an exploration of materials and process, as well as personal intent and conviction. That we can accept this duality is one of the most significant advances in design thinking since the Industrial Revolution, and we have Postmodernism to thank for unlocking the system.

In his excellent exhibition catalogue *Telling Tales: Fantasy and Fear in Contemporary Design*, Gareth Williams encapsulates the predominant characteristic of late 20th- and early 21st-century design: objects' ability to carry narrative meaning and associations. The following series of examples are by no means an exhaustive survey, nor are they meant to suggest formal 'groupings' of designers. Instead they simply offer a route through some of the narratives and interests in contemporary design.

TECHNO CRAFT

From the bent tubular steel, pliable woods and adhesives developed at the start of the 20th century, to the injection moulding of the 1960s and the rapid prototyping and stereo-lithography of more recent years, the histories of design have been built on increasing access to sophisticated materials and processes. However for some contemporary designers, the opportunities afforded by such extreme developments are still insufficient and only serve as formal exercises. Instead, they seek to marry poetry, craftsmanship and technology.

Rapid prototyping is perhaps the most radical fabrication technique of recent years – it has liberated design from the traditional designer-manufacturer relationship, and allows forms that were not previously possible without expensive tooling and moulds. Yet simply being able to produce a realised object in a minimal amount of time through expensive machinery does not justify an object's existence or expense.

As the designer Arik Levy argues, 'It's pretty poor that a material or a procedure makes the work good or not good. The procedure is part of the work and it's great that someone has researched and found out a way of using it, but come on, we are not inventing oxygen. You can say "It's very expensive because it took a $1,000,000 machine 48 hours to print." This I accept, but to say that it's an incredible piece because it took 48 hours on a $1,000,000 machine – excuse me!'[37]

The expectation that materials should look, feel and behave in specific ways has been overturned in recent years with the appropriation of composite materials from the ballistic and automotive industries. We think naturally of materials in clichés – fibres are soft, concrete is rigid – and expect their application to be limited to narrowly defined areas. Yet while Chris Kable's 'Seam' chair looks like it could crumple under the weight of its sitter, it is actually rigidly solid, challenging such preconceptions and usurping the clichés.

Marc Newson
Carbon ladder
2008

Carbon fibre, celebrated for its low weight and high strength, was developed for the aeronautic, space, automotive and sporting industries, where such strength-to-weight ratios are intrinsic to performance capacity. It is a material to which Marc Newson has constantly returned, his enthusiasm for which can be charted from the 'Black Hole' table (1988), to his Ford concept car (1999), the 'Mystery' clock (2000), the lightweight shells for the seats of his Qantas plane interiors and the 'Carbon fibre chair' (2008) produced for the Gagosian Gallery. However his 'Carbon' ladder for Galerie Kreo (2008) is perhaps Newson's shrewdest use of the material. A seemingly contemptible product choice for such a complex material – the simple ladder is the perfect conduit for the material's long list of virtues. At a sculpted 6ft tall, it weighs only 4.6lb, with each of its eight rungs capable of holding up to 220lb of weight.

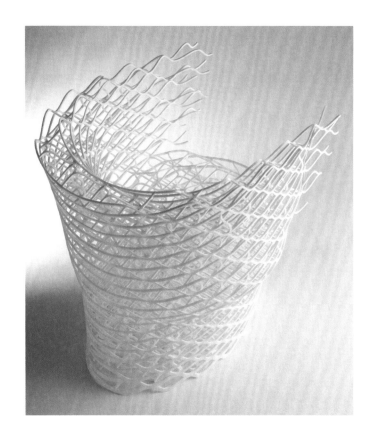

As its name suggests, rapid prototyping was developed as a way of producing prototypes for intricate components in the medical and automotive industries. A more accurate name for it is three-dimensional printing, as it transforms a computer-aided design into a 3D object by building the object layer by layer, working in the same way as an inkjet printer but creating solid forms out of liquid or powdered polymers, rather than just two-dimensional patterns.

This technique does not require expensive tooling and any conceivable shape can be produced. The possibilities offered by a tool that produces infinite quantities of identical objects with maximum simplicity and without additional costs are clearly tangible, but by tweaking the computer files, each object can be unique, suggesting the end of mass manufacturing.

Rapid prototyping, for all its virtues, can only produce objects up to a certain size. For the 'Diamond' chair, Nendo designed the chair as two pieces that snap together like a puzzle.

The 'Iris' table, by London-based designers Edward Barber and Jay Osgerby, marries high-precision manufacturing and hand-crafted production techniques. Informed by the Formula One automotive industry, each of the five different editions is constructed from a single component of machine-formed solid aluminium repeated to form a tessellated ring. Each of these single components has, through the anodising process, been hand-finished, thereby creating subtle differences between each table and capturing the beauty of a colour chart in a three-dimensional form.

Jeroen Verhoeven
Cinderella table
2005

The 'Cinderella' table harnesses both fine craftsmanship and high-tech manufacturing by shaping wood through computerised machinery. Verhoeven began by sketching the profiles of two different antique side tables – the front of one and the side of the other. He then digitised the sketches and used computer-aided design software to morph one shape onto the other, creating a virtual 3D hybrid form.

The computer file was sliced into 57 thin layers and translated to a CNC (computer numerically controlled) mill, which precisely cut each layer from a sheet of plywood to create complex compound curves. Verhoeven then glued the resulting 741 plywood layers together to create a solid object before sandpapering it.

Michael Eden
Wedgwoodn't tureen (tall pink)
2009

As an established maker of slip-decorated earthenware, Michael Eden's work shifted focus when he began investigating the potential of digital production methods in relation to traditional craft skills. There are only certain forms that a ceramicist can throw on a wheel; gravity, centrifugal force and the material qualities of clay limit the possibilities. By utilising rapid prototyping technologies, Eden was able to bypass these constraints to create entirely new forms that were once previously impossible to achieve. His 'Wedgwoodn't' tureen, described as 'the child of the new Industrial Revolution', acts as a commentary on the advances in production technology since the 18th century, when Josiah Wedgwood, the great industrialist, introduced new machines into his Etruria factory.

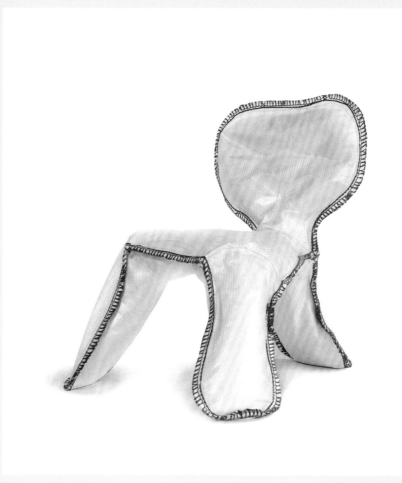

Chris Kabel
Seam chair
2007

Kable's 'Seam' chair was the by-product of a research project with the aerospace department of the Technical University in Delft and composites producer Lankhorst Indutech, which investigated the potential applications of Pure, a polypropylene woven fabric. Pure can be sewn rather than moulded to produce an infinite number of shapes at minimal cost. However, under the right pressure and certain temperatures, the soft fabric is transformed into a rigid structure. The process is comparable with the creation of resin and glass or carbon fibres, in which the outer core melts, impregnates and fixates the inner core. Unlike glass or carbon fibres, however, Pure is 100 percent recyclable and reusable.

FRANKENSTEIN DESIGN

Following the opening of Ron Arad's One Off studio-cum-gallery in London in 1981, his fellow designer and architect Nigel Coates likened the experience to visiting 'Dr Frankenstein's cave'.[58] So barbarian and post-apocalyptic were the works presented by Arad and his peers that they were later bestowed the title of 'post-industrial chic'.

Though not actively ecological in their remit, this group of like-minded designer-makers were employing easily sourced or found materials (steel tubing, scaffolding, architectural ironmongery) and workaday processes (hammering, welding, carving, hacking) out of economic necessity and a lack of support from the industry. While not a specifically unified movement, British-based designers such as Arad, alongside Tom Dixon and Danny Lane, shared a rebellious spirit in the face of the perceived reductiveness of Modernism and the industrial disputes of the 1970s.

These were works befitting a post-punk era which saw the rise of sampling spread throughout the music industry, but the idea of scavenging from the detritus of the everyday and sampling different disciplines and historical styles was not specific to the designer-makers of the 1980s. It has its precedents in Duchamp's urinal *Fountain* of 1917 and Achille and Pier Giacomo Castiglioni's 'Mezzadro' stool of 1957, made from a tractor seat.

The contemporary heirs to such cultural and industrial appropriations have not been driven so much by the desire for Dadaist shock, but a longing for design that has a relationship to the stuff of everyday life, reclaiming the individual's will to customise in an increasingly homogenised culture.

Ron Arad
Rover chair
1981

Tom Dixon
Victorian chair
1985

Tejo Remy
You Can't Lay Down Your Memory
chest of drawers, 1991

Fernando and Humberto Campana
Favela chair, 2003

Taking their cue from everyday scenarios and using unexpected combinations of found materials – such as rubber hose, tissue paper, string or furry toys – the brothers Fernando and Humberto Campana transform modest materials into objects that celebrate the discarded and mundane, and are instilled with the 'zest for life' of contemporary Brazil.

Committee
Big Brother
2005

Since founding Committee in 2001, Clare Page and Harry Richardson have
worked to apply pragmatism and imagination to exploring 'the drama of the
everyday'. At first glance, the colourful totems of skewered pottery animals,
vases, figurines, boxes and other bric-a-brac of their 'Kebab' lamps look like
a cheerful jumble of random objects. However, the choice and the sequences
of objects were meticulously considered in order to explore a theme or to tell
a story, and consequently each lamp is a unique sculpture, filled with pieces
from different eras that allude to the constant turning of fashion and style and
the flow of objects into and out of our lives. 'Big Brother', for example, muses
on the often threatening power of omnipresent CCTV surveillance. Their work
comes as much from the Dadaist beginnings of the found object as an attempt
to find a practical solution to a problem, but is also a deliberate reaction
against the slick form-making of much contemporary design.

Stuart Haygarth
Tide
2005

To a child, a plastic doll can hold as much beauty as one made from china. A fragment of cut glass is just as attractive to the magpie as a diamond. Finding enjoyment or splendour in that which is cheap, colourful or shiny should not be considered simple-minded or in bad taste but instead just simple and sincere.

Elevating the commonplace or discarded object is a central tenant of Stuart Haygarth's work. Having shifted from commercial photography to product design in 2005, Haygarth's exquisite lighting designs have employed the flotsam and jetsam of everyday life – from man-made debris washed up on the seashore to hundreds of salvaged prescription spectacles. As he has said, 'my work revolves around everyday objects, collected in large quantities, categorised and presented in such a way that they are given new meaning. It is about giving banal and overlooked objects new significance.'

Martino Gamper
If Giò only Knew
2007

Martino Gamper's work has been characterised by spontaneity and the collapse of the processes of design and making. Gamper's '100 chairs 100 days' project (illustrated opposite) involved collecting discarded chairs from London streets (or more frequently, friends' homes) over a two-year period, then spending 100 days to reconfigure the design of each one in an attempt to transform its character or the way it functions. Gamper investigates the potential for creating useful new designs by blending elements of existing chair types. Due to the time constraints, the chairs were put together with a minimum of analysis, like a subconscious act of appropriation, though Gamper used these mongrel forms to demonstrate the difficulty of any particular design being objectively judged 'the best'.

Martino Gamper
100 chairs 100 days
2007

Rolf Sachs
Tailor Made
2008

Liliana Ovalle
Mugroso
2006

CRITICAL DESIGN

Critical Design, as outlined by its key proponents, the interactive designers and educators Anthony Dunne and Fiona Raby, is design that uses the mechanisms of its industry to question and challenge industrial agendas; embody alternative social, cultural, technical or economic values; and act as a prop to stimulate debate and discussion amongst the public, designers and industry.

Design has always acted as a barometer of cultural desires, technological advances and market strategies. However such readings have normally been outward in their vision. One of Critical Design's remits is to critique the industry itself. Beyond Dunne and Raby, there is no formal grouping of these designers, only an ambivalent, critical position and the spirited, playful language used to express this.

Design as critique has existed before. Throughout the 1960s and 1970s – a time of mass strikes and student riots in Europe – both artists and designers were exploring political concerns, often anti-consumerism, in their work as members of the Arte Povera and Anti-Design movements. Building on such manifestos, contemporary Critical Design is a response to the world we live in today. The exponents believe that our social relations, desires, fantasies, hopes and fears are very different from those at the beginning of the 20th century, yet many key ideas informing mainstream design stem form that period. Society, they believe, has moved on, but design has not. Critical Design is one of many mutations design is undergoing in an effort to remain relevant to the complex technological, political, economic and social changes we are experiencing at the beginning of the 21st century.

The growing interest in Critical Design has been reflected in the number of exhibitions dealing with this emerging genre over recent years including London's Architecture Foundation's *Don't Panic: Emergent Critical Design* in 2007, *Designing Critical Design* at Belgium's Z33 gallery in 2007, *Wouldn't It Be Nice … Wishful Thinking in Art and Design*, 2007, at the Centre d'Art Contemporain, Geneva, and *Design and The Elastic Mind*, 2008, at the Museum of Modern Art, New York.

Martí Guixé
Skip furniture
2004

Dunne & Raby with Michael Anastassiades
Priscila Huggable Atomic Mushroom
2004

Dunne and Raby's designs defy authority and challenge reality, conveying a view of the world that, although positive and hopeful, may at first be disquieting. 'Huggable Atomic Mushroom', part of a series titled 'Designs for Fragile Personalities in Anxious Times', is modelled on the mushroom cloud created by the detonation of a 37-kiloton test bomb in Nevada in 1957. As the series title suggests, the objects offer a means of coping with fear that falls between denial and paranoia. This variation on an anxiety-relief cushion allows people to confront the neurosis of war by turning a horrific event into a domestic and huggable object.

Gruppo Strum
Pratone seating
1966–70

Founded in 1963 by architects Giorgio Ceretti, Pietro Derossi, Carla Giammarco, Riccardo Rosso and Maurizio Vogliazzo, Gruppo Strum interpreted the built environment as the platform from which they could participate in the social and political protests of the time. Inspired by the over-sized and out-of-context Pop Art sculptures of Claes Oldenburg, 'Pratone' was an allegory of the collective pastoral longing which grew during the late 1960s, as part of the radical protest against consumer society. Constructed from cold-foamed polyurethane, painted with green varnish, 'Pratone' was a featured exhibit in the Museum of Modern Art's 1972 seminal exhibition *Italy: The New Domestic Landscape*, in which the curator Emilio Ambasz positioned a wide range of conflicting theories about the state of design, architecture and urban development and the growing distrust of objects of consumption.

Alessandro Mendini
Proust armchair
1978

Studio Alchimia, formed in 1976 in Milan, created conceptual ideas that mixed Modernism with mysticism and the banality of daily life, which were disseminated through publications and exhibitions, notably the Venice Biennale of 1980. Its members included Ettore Sottsass and Alessandro Mendini, who was the editor of the design journal *Modo* and the group's chief theorist. They played games with decoration as a subversive attack on the prevailing notions of 'good taste'. Mendini's 'Proust' armchair was the first physical manifestation of their theories on the kitsch and banal in design, though the group's rejection of consumerism precluded any large-scale production.

Jurgen Bey sees himself as a researcher who analyses the world we live in, with the aim of discovering the hidden qualities, stories and emotional value of objects. With his architect partner Rianne Makkink, Bey is preoccupied with concepts of lightness, both in terms of reducing the weight of materials and cutting down on the need for transportation, as explored through the 'Crate' cabinets project (overleaf), launched in 2003–4 and revisited in 2008 for an exhibition at Mitterand & Cramer in Geneva. His 'PROOFF' range of products was designed to help make offices more inspiring places to be. Most of these products, like the 'Earchair', were originally intended to solve specific problems for individual clients, such as the need for absolute privacy within a crowded public space.

Studio Makkink and Bey
Crate cabinets
2008

Architects had this great moment of evolving when they could hardly build anything. This was a paper architecture period where architects wrote a lot and developed incredible model making. [Rem] Koolhaas was making all these models that were quite abstract, expressions – almost like art. I think design also needs this period. Not that we shouldn't be making things, but in the sense of finding a way to develop its course. We need good debate.

Jurgen Bey, designer, Rotterdam[59]

WOKmedia
Once
2008

Responding to the incredible waste of natural products, WOKmedia's Julie Mathias and Wolfgang Kaeppner have designed a furniture series called 'Once', constructed entirely of inexpensive wooden chopsticks. It is estimated that China produces more than 45 billion chopsticks a year, which are used once and then thrown away; to make them requires the wood of 25 million fully grown trees. To draw attention to this, Mathias and Kaeppner created chairs, stools and tables out of thousands of recycled chopsticks. These are dropped into a stack that, because of the huge number of interlacing sticks, supports the weight of a person. Two humble splints of wood, designed to be snapped apart before use and discarded after a meal, have become a symbol of monumental waste in a world of depleting resources.

PERFORMATIVE DESIGN

In recent years, the narrative-led agenda of 1990s design has been subtly restructured. In its place has emerged a group of designers who are treating the entire design process as a live performance – creating form not by sketching or modelling, but through real-time events witnessed live or through film. Consequently, the objects start to tell the story of their creation, with the focus shifting from the autonomous, finished work to the process of the object's evolution.

Unlike the near-century-old practice of performance art, this is a relatively new phenomenon for contemporary design. It is driven by many factors, including a growing enthusiasm to breach disciplinary boundaries, the ease and speed with which designers' dramatic exploits can be disseminated over the internet, and the increasing proliferation of design blogs.

Marcus Fairs, the editor of the design blog *Dezeen*, suggests that 'such telegenic acts of creation confirm that the design process can be as pleasing – or as provocative – an aesthetic experience as the designed object itself. As avant-garde design enters a new, post-functional phase – in which the cultural or emotional value of an object is equal to, or greater than, its functional value – so designers are liberated to pioneer such new routes to form.'[50]

Performance-led design is not without its antecedents. The Italian artist and designer Bruno Munari believed that anyone could produce objects of aesthetic value, given the proper technological advantages. To this end he began installing photocopiers at exhibition sites, including one in the Central Pavilion of the 35th Venice Biennale in 1970. Rather than impose their performances on existing objects, contemporary designers are using the performance to actually create their objects; the documentation of the process is just as important as the results of this labour. As Sarah van Gameran of Studio Glithero has said, 'there is a double spotlight: one on the end product and one of the process; without the timeline they cannot exist.'[51]

Max Lamb
Pewter stool
2006

If you see Max Lamb with his feet in the sand, labouring away with molten pewter – you immediately realise that there is a lot more going on than producing a chair for Ikea. This is about process, unpredictability, exploration, difficulty and resolution. It's something unique, something to be celebrated and that only comes across when witnessing the act of creation.

Ambra Medda, director, Design Miami/

Maarten Baas
Real Time
2009–10

Maarten Baas chose the language of cinema to redesign the clock. The passing of time is represented by films depicting the changing minutes, screened in a true interval of 12 or 24 hours. The 'Real Time' series (above and opposite) encompassed four scenarios: the old-style grandfather clock (the clock face is a screen showing a film of the hands being drawn); the sweeper clock (the hands are formed by two people sweeping lines of rubbish); the analogue digital (a video shows LED dashes being either painted in, to make them visible, or wiped clean); the world clock (people from three different countries were filmed indicating the local time, re-arranging objects in front of them as the hands of a clock).

Atelier NL.
Sleeping Beauty
2006

By making products and prototypes in situ, designers introduce a temporal apect to their work. Atelier NL's 'Sleeping Beauty' lamp (which knits its own hood), or Studio Glithero's 'Running Mould' benches (made by forcing wet plaster through a large pincer time and time again until the plaster completely cures) and their Panta Rei candle-making machine are three examples that show a certain fascination with mechanical processes revealing themselves over time. Capturing the spontaneity of performance-led design is also possible through rapid prototyping, or 'fabbing', as it is known. The Front Design team developed a unique method by which freehand sketches materialise into form using the motion capture technologies established in the computer animation and video gaming industries. The designers sketch the form of a chair, table, lamp, whatever in the air and these movements are recorded with motion-capture video technology, before being digitised into a 3D computer model. The digital files are then sent to a rapid manufacturing machine that uses computer-controlled lasers to print the objects in plastic, allowing the first tentative sketch to become the final product.

Studio Glithero
Panta Rei/Everything Flows
2008

Studio Glithero
Running Mould
2010

Front
Sketch furniture
2005

rAndom International
with Chris O'Shea
Audience, 2008

The design team of rAndom International have also sought to immerse
the public in the realisation of their designs. 'Audience', an installation
commissioned by choreographer Wayne McGregor in 2008 for a performance
at the Royal Opera House in London, consists of a large crowd of floor-based,
head-sized mirrors on motorised rotating arms. When members of the
audience enter the perimeter of the installation, the mirrors inquisitively select
a person to follow. Having chosen a subject, the mirrors synchronise and turn
their 'heads' towards that person, reflecting the subject back and forth across
the installation space. The installation reverses the roles of the viewer and the
viewed. When the mirrors ignore the subject, the person involved often starts
performing to get their attention back.

Paul Cocksedge
Kiss
2009

In performance-led design, the locus can be the physical body of the designer, the object itself or the space surrounding the object. It reflects a keen desire to explore the 'situational' and 'relational' aspects of the object, its installation or environment and relies heavily on the direct participation of the public, be it in such seemingly banal tasks as eating or kissing. For designer Paul Cocksedge's installation 'Kiss', a vast LED canopy was designed to cover the interior dome of the Galleria Vittorio Emanuele II in Milan. From this canopy, a large artificial mistletoe was suspended above a stage for visitors to indulge in the European tradition of kissing under it. The physical meeting of the couple's lips acted like an electrical conductor, activating a lighting sequence which illuminated the canopy and consequently the entire central atria of the Galleria, making an intimate moment a very public spectacle.

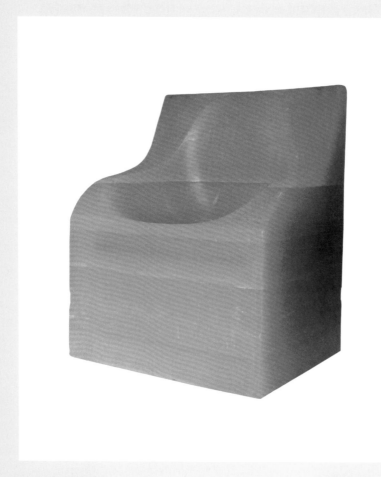

**Julia Lohmann and
Gero Grundmann**
Erosion armchair, 2007

Objects have the ability to develop, grow or evolve after leaving the design studio. The designer does not deliver a static and fully defined product but instead offers an object in flux where external agents – such as nature or the end user – supervise its final form. In this, the object becomes the actor on the stage, and the process of creation becomes part of an unfolding drama.

The 'Erosion' series by Julia Lohmann and Gero Grundmann was made from industrially sourced glycerine – soap. The high moisture content of the soap slowly sweats from the object, requiring the owner to keep constant vigil by wiping away the excess moisture. Through this intervention, the owner actively erodes the object's form. The moisture will eventually evaporate and the object will reach petrification, but in the process the owner will have altered the final form.

Frank Tjepkema and Peter Van der Jagt

Do Break, 2000

'Do Break' by Frank Tjepkema and Peter Van der Jagt was designed as part of the 'Do Create' range from Droog collection – objects on which the user was invited to leave their mark. The vase comes with instructions encouraging the buyer to smash the vase: on impact, the rubber lining holds the porcelain fragments together while the decorative cracks that appear as pattern act as a permanent reminder of the dramatic moment.

SCIENCE, NATURE AND DESIGN

From the nano-molecular to the macro mega-structural scale, science has long been a source of inspiration for the conceptual framework and process of design. Fractal geometries, physics, biomimicry and biotechnologies, to name but a few, have been harvested and harnessed by designers looking to engage their work with the advancing world around them. For some, it's a celebration of nature's law in the creation of mathematically perfect and complex forms. For others, it is a theoretical application of laboratory-based research and development to simulate growth, development, irregular regularity and repetition.

The core strength of certain natural cell configurations, such as the honeycomb pattern, has been adapted by the design and architecture industries for millennia. Charles Darwin described the honeycomb as a masterpiece of efficient engineering that is 'absolutely perfect in economising labour and wax'. From Frank Gehry's 'Easy Edges' cardboard furniture range of 1971 to Tokujin Yoshioka's glassine paper 'Honey Pop' chair of 2001, the tensile structures offered by honeycomb have given rise to a variety of low-cost, but highly valued, lightweight constructions with strong resistance to vertical compression.

'Honeycomb' vase by Tomáš Gabzdil Libertiny is a direct practical examination of nature's role in design. In a process he described as 'slow prototyping', Libertiny placed a specially crafted vase-shaped mould in a beehive, then patiently waited while an estimated 40,000 bees built the layered honeycomb vase simulacrum within the formal constraints of the mould. The vase is the appropriate form for Libertiny's studies: 'the material comes from the flowers as a by-product of bees, and ends up serving the flowers on their last journey.'[53]

As software coding has caught up with our understanding of nature's own codes – such as the flocking patterns of birds – designers have been able to forge a meeting of mathematics and natural processes in their designs. It is not always a random act of growth, but sometimes a predetermined translation of innate patterns into process and form.

We're in such an era of flux, one that is characterised by hybridisation and exploration and innovation, and obviously science and digitalisation.

Zoë Ryan, Neville Bryan Curator of Design, Art Institute of Chicago[54]

Frank O. Gehry
Easy Edges Wiggle side chair
1971

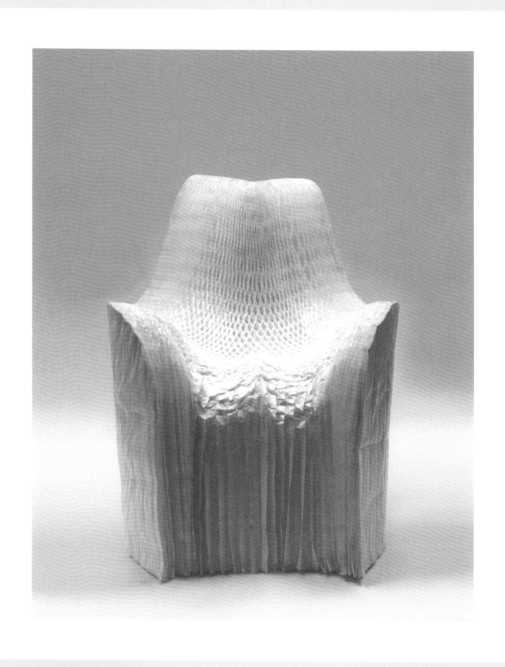

Tokujin Yoshioka
Honey Pop
2001

Tokujin Yoshioka
Venus Natural chair
2008

Japanese designer Tokujin Yoshioka explored the chance patterns born from nature's beauty through his 'Venus Natural' chair which was literally grown in a tank and emerged from the waters like the goddess Venus, as a fully-formed crystalline structure. A basic chair-shaped mesh of soft polyester fibres, acting as a substrate, was lowered into a solution-filled aquarium. Minerals were melted into the solution and began attaching themselves to the fibres, and the resulting crystal growth formed the chair's structure.

Studio Libertiny
Honeycomb vase, Made by Bees
2006

Joris Laarman
Bone chair
2010

Beginning with his first 'Bone' chairs of 2006, Laarman's highly sculptural forms are based on an algorithm originally developed by the German scientist Claus Matthek to reveal the regenerative capacity of human bone and tree growth. Matthek's algorithm was later adopted by Opal, the German automotive company, to craft car parts that were optimised both for strength and for minimal material use. Laarman's 'Bone' series of furniture is similarly crafted into a series of bone or branch forms that offer load-bearing support where needed and open voids where no material is required. In his own words, he sculpted 'using mother nature's underlying codes'.

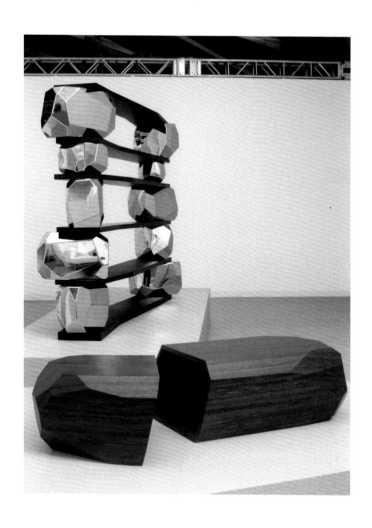

Whether crafted from relentlessly polished stainless steel so as to resemble seamlessly mirrored boulders, or wooden polygonal structures reminiscent of petrified logs, when presented in a domestic setting Arik Levy's 'Rock' series recalls nature, but are only vague appropriations of nature. By subverting convention through material choice and scale, Levy presents nature out of context – luring the viewer with false securities then confounding them with the contradictions inherent in their own expectations. It's a perverse reminder of mankind's impact on the natural world but also of Levy's fascination with absence, 'empty instead of full, lightweight instead of heavy, belonging to the human mind instead of nature.'[55]

Simon Heijdens
Lightweeds
2006

Simon Heijdens's immersive installations employ digital media to reveal how we relate to the spaces and objects around us, how that relationship evolves over the course of a day or a season. As an antidote to the immutable and unresponsive built environment, Heijdens imposes bespoke software programming and various sensors to natural processes, creating 'living digital organisms'. Heijdens's digital plant forms mature and grow in response to externally monitored information – be that the shifting weather conditions outside, or the periodic movements inside the room. As the plant's behavioural patterns are directly derived from this continuously collected data, the logic of nature is brought into the artificial world.

Julia Lohmann
Ruminant Bloom
2004

Ayala Serfaty
Soma
2009

ENTROPY

Entropy is the scientific principle stating that all systems become increasingly chaotic with time – or more simply, it describes nature's abhorrence of uniformity. In design, entropy can be used as an umbrella term to describe the increasing number of practitioners exploring ways of introducing chaos, decay and error into their work.

This development can be seen as a deliberate reaction against, on the one hand, the long-valued characteristics of timelessness and perfection as upheld by established models of manufacturing, and on the other the absolute precision of digital design and advanced production processes. It is therefore only natural that the reaction against conventional manufacturing should be to make things that glory in flaws and imperfections and value endless, almost random variation.

One name in particular dominates: Gaetano Pesce, the New York-based artist and designer who has spent nearly 50 years happily defying conventional notions of good taste, producing a body of work that is often unattractive, and always provocative and interesting. 'We want something human [in design],' says Pesce. 'And the only way is to introduce the "badly done" into things. The bad realisation, the version with mistakes, it gives the object a soul. And at that moment, what we were calling ugly, it becomes beautiful because it's carrying human qualities that abstract beauty cannot carry.'[55]

Computer-based designers such as Reed Kram and Clemens Weisshaar are experimenting with digital entropy through their 'Breeding' tables, developing algorithms that lead to a degree of unpredictability in the final (computer-manufactured) object. Dutch designer Hella Jongerius's pieces deliberately show traces of how they were made, embracing imperfections and unusual mixtures of materials and techniques.

This idea of embedding value or personalisation in the work is also taken on by Simon Heijdens. When new, the cups, bowls and plates in his 'Broken White' ceramics series are perfectly white and smooth. As each piece is used, delicate cracks appear in the glazing – and a pattern of flowers seems to grow across the surface. Heijdens achieved this effect by manipulating the traditional technique of craquelure glazing to ensure that the appearance of each piece changes from the moment of use. As the extent of crackling is determined by the frequency of use, each piece rapidly assumes a distinctive character with favourite – or most used – objects becoming the most decorative.

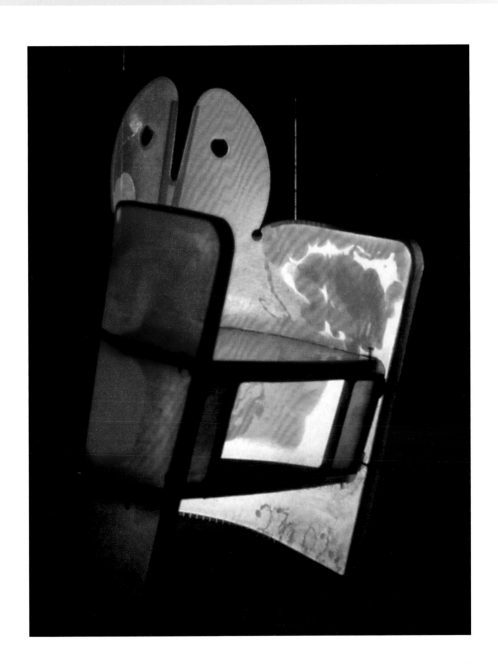

Gaetano Pesce
Nobody's Perfect
2002

Kram Weisshaar
Breeding tables
2003 ongoing

Hella Jongerius
Soft urns
1994

Simon Heijdens
Broken White
2004

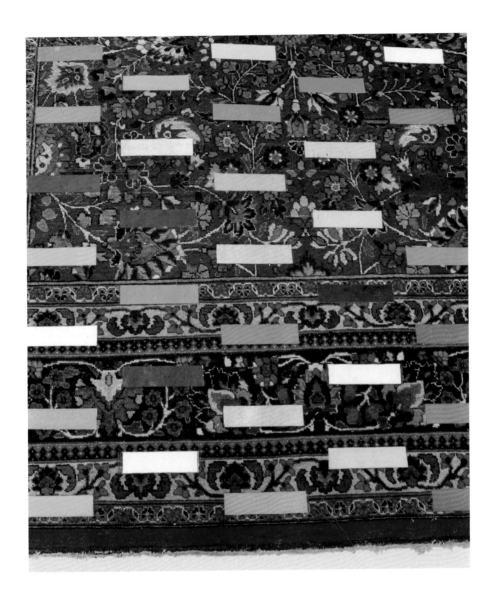

Bertjan Pot
Duct Tape carpet
2009

Whenever I find a good rug that I think I can improve with some duct-tape colours, I buy them and mangle them in this way. The duct-tape is really molten into the textile so it won't come off when using it as a carpet.

Bertjan Pot, designer, Rotterdam[57]

(RE)INVENTING DESIGN TYPOLOGIES

Most designs are variations on an existing form. Rarely are new typologies of products developed. Perhaps this says more about the overdevelopment of our contemporary society than it does about the ingenuity of designers; however, among the handful of practitioners who are challenging this status quo are the French brothers Ronan and Erwan Bouroullec.

While it is impossible to erase the influence of all that has come before, the Bouroullec brothers seek a new design language and different type of logic to the accepted norm. As Gareth Williams, former Curator of the Victoria and Albert Museum and now Senior Tutor at the Royal College of Art, has said: 'At its best, the Bouroullecs' work contains a balanced tension between absolute control of their medium and total disrespect for convention.'[53] At the core of their creative process is the continual questioning of how we actually live our lives. Through flexibility and modularity, their designs respond to our 21st-century desire for constant change, allowing the user to customise their environment as circumstances change, or their wishes demand.

While they are only in their thirties, the Bouroullecs' quiet revolutions in design have been felt across the industry. In keeping with their philosophy of adaptability and efficiency even where design typologies are not entirely new, the function given to certain objects has been rethought. The traditional 'fit for purpose' mantra that assigned one function to one object has been broken down by contemporary designers who are looking to offer a wider range of experiences from both the production and consumption of design. After all, the form of an iPhone is not necessarily driven by its function – communication tool, computer, camera, dictionary, calculator, spirit level, blackjack machine...

Ronan and Erwan Bouroullec

Lit Clos, 2000

Fredrikson Stallard
Pyrenees sofa
2007

Léon de Lange
Karakters
2008

Lotty Lindeman
Tassenkast
2009

Ronan and Erwan Bouroullec
Lianes, 2010

EXTERNAL INFLUENCES

CASE STUDY

MARC NEWSON, 'LOCKHEED LOUNGE'

In the weeks leading up to the April 2009 Phillips de Pury auction in London, in which Marc Newson's 'Lockheed Lounge' held centre stage, one dealer described the aluminium chaise as the 'seminal piece of contemporary design' against which 'everything in the market is measured'; certainly the auction results didn't disappoint despite the concerns of the economic recession. In the swoop of a gavel, the 'Lockheed Lounge' upgraded its status from one of the most discussed and coveted design objects of the last few decades to holder of the world-record auction price for a work by living designer, exceeding its £500,000–£700,000 presale estimate to sell for £1,105,250.

Such is the perceived power of this piece that rarely is an article about collecting design published in which the 'Lockheed Lounge' is not cited. Meanwhile, Marc Newson's own importance outside the sphere of design was formally acknowledged when *Time* magazine named him one of the 100 most influential people in the world.[69]

Yet all of this seems a long way away from the humble origins of the 'Lockheed Lounge' in the mid-1980s, when Newson spent 'a couple of miserable months' solving the design process. His intention had been to cover its fibreglass core, shaped using traditional surfboard-making practices, with a single sheet of aluminium: 'I tried laminating it, but the thing fell apart... eventually, I came up with the idea of beating little pieces of metal into shape with a wooden mallet and attaching them with rivets.'[70]

Although marked by the limitations of a young designer working outside of the support system of industrial production, the 'Lockheed Lounge' was, and is still, deserving of the accolade it receives – it is a stunningly seductive and extraordinary object within which lies the genesis of Newson's success. But an exploration of these factors (tangible or otherwise; intentional or otherwise; inherent or applied) suggests that there is more to the 'Lockheed Lounge' and its subsequent chartered success than the celebration of a beautiful object.

Marc Newson's reputation as one of the most accomplished and influential designers of his generation is deserved. Born in Sydney in 1963, he spent a peripatetic childhood travelling through Australia, Asia and Europe, before returning to study sculpture and jewellery design at Sydney College of the Arts. Within a year of graduation he was invited to exhibit with Roslyn Oxley's Sydney gallery in June 1986. Amongst the handful of objects created specifically for the exhibition, Newson exhibited the 'LC1' chaise-longue (a precursor to the 'Lockheed Lounge'), which was subsequently purchased by the Art Gallery of South Australia for an alleged A$3,000. From Australia he travelled to Japan in 1987 where a fortuitous meeting with the influential design retailer, manufacturer and patron Teruo Kurosaki resulted in Newson's works filtering out to a wider audience attracting the attention of international media and manufacturer alike.

In just over two decades, since his graduation in 1985, Newson has traversed the global spectrum of design disciplines to create furniture, interiors, watches, objects, domestic appliances and editioned works, as well as large-scale contracts for the transport industry – notably bicycles, a concept car, a private jet and a space-plane for space tourism. He is artistic director of Qantas and has designed the airport lounges and interiors of the entire fleet, including the A380 Airbus. His client list ranges through Europe, North America, Asia and Australia, and his futuristically fluid and organic forms have influenced a raft of copycat products and designers alike.

He has exhibited in galleries and public institutions including Fondation Cartier pour l'Art Contemporain, Paris (1995, 2004); Powerhouse Museum, Sydney (2001), London's Design Museum (2004–5) and the Gagosian Gallery, New York (2007). His designs are present in most major museum collections including the Museum of Modern Art in New York, London's Design Museum, the Pompidou Centre and the Vitra Design Museum. And there are few international design awards and accolades that Newson has not won.

Throughout all Newson's accomplishments, from his early postgraduate works through to the unveiling of his suborbital jet designed for EADS Astrium in Paris or the highly sculptural editioned designs for Gagosian Gallery, there has been a consistent visual language. Newson has claimed he can't see this signature style, being too close to the work – yet it is this authorial tone, the visible hand of the artist, that makes his work so desirable. It also liberates his work from any specific moment in design history, rendering projects timeless as they retain their vibrancy and validity.

As Newson has acknowledged, 'Australia has a history of invention driven by necessity.' His early studies of jewellery and sculpture were driven by both lack and need: the lack of an available degree in design that could satisfy his need to learn how to 'make things: how to lathe, how to weld ... how to make things the way I wanted to make them.'[71] It was during this period that Newson's alchemist's understanding of materials was established; he cites Oppi Untracht's *Metal Techniques for Craftsmen* (New York: Robert Hale, 1968) as the text that exposed him to cultures and techniques beyond his own. Ever since, Newson has approached design as an exercise in extreme structures and advanced technologies, combining a highly tactile and exacting exploration of materials, processes, and skills. Beyond the practical lessons learned from his jewellery training, Newson also established at this early stage an appreciation of designing for the human form. His appreciation of furniture as jewellery for the body belies a sculptural sensibility that has consequently drawn parallels between the 'Lockheed Lounge' and Alexander Archipenko's *Torso in Space* of 1936. To this extent Newson has continually returned to the hourglass shape first developed in the 'Lockheed Lounge' for much of his subsequent work, including the 'Pod' drawers (1987), the 'Embryo' chair (1988), 'Orgone' lounges (1989) and the 'Rock' doorstop produced by Magis (1997).

Named in homage to the machine-age aesthetic of the American aircraft manufacturer, the 'Lockheed Lounge' was imbued with a sequence of subtle yet highly personal influences. That Newson chose to model the 'Lockheed' as a chaise-longue, a relatively outmoded furniture type in the late 20th century, pinpointed his unique position outside of any existing aesthetical movement, while establishing the now-frequently cited influences of Neoclassicism, Postmodernism, the space race and surf culture – references to which he has ceaselessly returned.

Reflected against the monochrome linear geometry of corporate 1980s design, the 'Lockheed' persists as a solitary example of organic design. It has been claimed that the 'Lockheed Lounge' brought the aesthetic vocabulary of 21st-century design

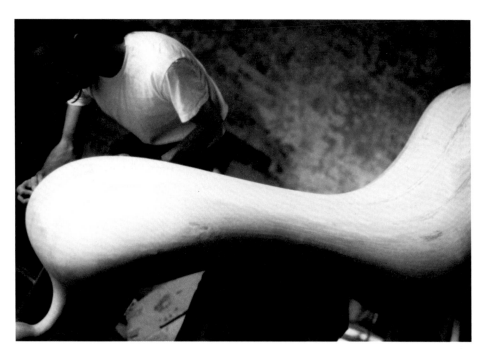

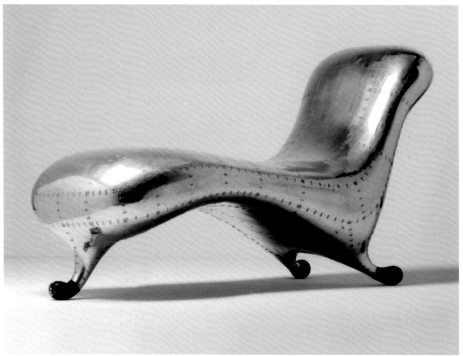

into being. Its timing was perfect. While Newson may not have been making or indeed selling the work in volume during the late 1980s and early 1990s, it was certainly being copiously devoured by a hungry horde of nascent lifestyle magazines and their readers, all eager for photogenic design-porn.

Newson was good copy for the press – a young Australian designer who had shrugged off the tyranny of distance to bring his rigorously executed though glamorously relaxed designs to an international market. His long ponytail, his forays into modelling for fashion label Comme des Garçons, his passion for classic cars and beautiful women – some of these might be media myth, but it was these constructs that brought Newson's work to the wider audience and added a perceived extra layer of allure to his work.

An early and enthusiastic supporter was Philippe Starck, who in 1990 acquired an example of the 'Lockheed Lounge' for the lobby of Ian Schrager's Paramount Hotel in New York. Situated centre-stage in the hippest hotel of the time, and with endorsement from both Starck and Schrager, this was the next stepping-stone to success. Then, in 1993 the 'Lockheed' was brought to an ever-wider audience when it featured in the video for Madonna's single 'Rain'. Now the MTV generation had access to Newson's work. Two years later, Vitra Design Museum included the 'Lockheed' in their highly influential travelling exhibition of *100 Masterpieces*, and in 2000 the chaise was the focus of the Carnegie Art Museum's aluminium retrospective. Finally high culture, pop culture and academia had formally embraced the 'Lockheed Lounge'.

By 2000, when Christie's and Sotheby's were spearheading their respective campaigns to bring design into the auction house, the 'Lockheed Lounge' – now in an edition of 10 with four artist's proofs – was the holy grail of lots, with each of the houses fighting to have the next rare sighting of the lounge in their auction. And each of them did. One of the examples was sold at Christie's in 2000 for $105,000. Just six years later, another sold for almost $1 million, then reappeared in a gallery a few months later with a price tag of $2.5 million. In 2007, Christie's established the record at $1.5 million, then Phillips de Pury exceeded all records in April 2009 and will offer another lounge at auction in 2010. In 23 years, the 'Lockheed Lounge' had gone from A$3,000 to £1.1 million.

As Alexander Payne, worldwide director of design for Phillips de Pury, modestly stated at the time of the 2009 sale, 'we are extremely pleased with the results of this sale.' He added, 'Marc Newson is a stellar designer who has made an indelible contribution to design and the "Lockheed Lounge" is a seminal piece. It deserves the price that it achieved. The total result of the sale bears witness to the fact that the market for important and rare pieces of international design continues to grow. It was the result of much hard work to present a consistently top-quality offering, and the market responded.'[73]

It would be a misrepresentation to conclude that the 'Lockheed Lounge' has maintained its iconic status purely as a result of mythmaking, savvy litigation, and marketing. Newson's early design for an aluminium lounge is stunning, it is timeless and it does belie the genesis of his design vocabulary – technical rigour, futurism and aerodynamic fluidity.

Today we have a system of supply and demand. That doesn't bother me. Take Marc Newson's famous 'Lockheed Lounge'... it's a work of art, it is priceless, and it will still be in 100 years.

Marcel Brient, collector, Paris[74]

HOW

_____

WHAT I FIND ABOUT MOST COLL-
ECTORS IS THAT THEY REALLY
KNOW THEIR STUFF; THEY'RE
ALMOST DOING THEIR OWN
PHD. THEY TRAVEL THE WORLD
LOOKING FOR WHATEVER
THEY ARE INTERESTED IN
AND THEY BECOME FASCIN-
ATED WITH A PARTICULAR
THING, WHETHER IT'S FROM
A PARTICULAR PERIOD,
OR FROM A PARTICULAR
AREA.THEY NOT ONLY KNOW
THE HISTORY OF THE PIECE,
BUT ALSO WHEN IT WENT INTO
AUCTION, HOW MUCH IT SOLD
FOR (OR DIDN'T SELL FOR) AND
OFTEN EVEN WHOM IT SOLD
TO. THEY SEE IT AS A SERIOUS
HOBBY WITH A BUSINESS SIDE.

A collector's success is directly proportionate to how much time they put into research and education. Whether they choose to collect from galleries, auction houses or direct from the designer, the overriding recommendation is to explore their interests and these varied markets, establish lasting relationships with their points of contact in each of the fields and participate or attend key events and exhibitions throughout the year.

GALLERIES AND DEALERS

Collecting design from galleries is not a new phenomenon: Eileen Gray sold work by her peers in a Paris gallery in the 1920s, while antique galleries have been dealing design for centuries. However, contemporary-design galleries have been under the spotlight in recent years, as they explore the opportunities that the new directions in design are affording them.

For all its narrative and cultural layering, contemporary design often needs a space to articulate its symbolic function – something a retail environment could never offer, with all the visual chatter from other merchandise. The gallery environment offers a platform for this engagement and reflection.

For the collector, the growing number of galleries that specialise in design has increased access to collectible design, not just in physical terms but also in awareness and information. With the rise in galleries specialising in collectible design has come a concurrent interest from the media, and a wealth of articles and books and specialist magazines have emerged in tandem.

CHOOSING A GALLERY

Most gallerists are collectors in their own right, so they perceive their professional role as an extension of their private passion. Virtually all of them have a long history of involvement in the profession – some have come from the art world, others from the antiques world, some from the manufacturing industry and others from museums and institutions. Whatever their origins, all are 100 percent committed and passionate about their profession; this expertise and knowledge is a valuable asset for a collector to tap in to.

I can think of some galleries who have taken quite a risk in commissioning collections of work from particular designers that would be potentially a tough sell. With the shift of time and hindsight, you could argue that the good galleries, although taking a risk at the time, were setting the agenda for the future and helping to move things forward. The whole question of timing and trying to broaden the new is a very important dynamic.

Ben Evans, director, London Design Festival[75]

The market for collecting is divided into primary and secondary markets. The former refers to contemporary works that are being sold for the first time. The latter could be either contemporary or historical works, on the market for a second or subsequent time. Sometimes, however, a dealer can work between both primary and secondary markets. It's an interesting model as it allows the collector an opportunity to see works from different periods in one spectrum, informing and inspiring an eclectic selection.

Primary gallerists are the main conduits for contemporary works. Their role is to source, secure, support and sell works by designers, which have either been made specifically for the gallery or have been taken into the gallery direct from the designer's studio. The important word to stress here is 'support', as the primary market gallery is more than just a space to sell (indeed, some galleries operate without formal venues) – it is the platform from which a designer's future career is guided, documented and sustained.

Even art galleries have, in recent years, started including works by designers amongst their collections – witness the examples of Timothy Taylor (Ron Arad), Emmanuel Perrotin (Eric Benque, José Levy, Robert Stadler), Haunch of Venison (Thomas Heatherwick, Stuart Haygarth, Demakersvan) and Gagosian (Marc Newson). That the recent economic recession did not entirely kill off this market suggests that the strength and stability of design galleries will continue. As more primary dealers emerge, the market will continue to mature and broaden into other areas beyond furniture. Galleries have already embraced the rich heritage of graphic design, with Deitch

Projects in New York presenting the work of Stefan Sagmeister in 2008; the British designer Peter Saville showing at Galerie Neu in Berlin in 2005; and M/M (Paris) at London's Haunch of Venison in 2006 and the Pompidou Centre in 2007.

Digital design, too, has been highlighted through museum exhibitions such as *Design and the Elastic Mind* at the Museum of Modern Art, New York, in 2008 and *Decode* at the Victoria and Albert Museum in 2010. In London, commercial galleries such as Carpenter's Workshop and my own, Gallery Libby Sellers, have supported interactive and new-media designers such as rAndom International, Simon Heijdens and Daniel Brown, while in New York Bitforms gallery has supported Daniel Rozin and Golan Levin.

You have to be really on the hunt, and you have to also love the hunt. There's that passion ... that quest. It can be done.

Brian Kish, dealer, New York"

EXCLUSIVITY AND SALES

Unlike the relationships between most fine artists and galleries, which is generally one based on exclusive rights for the relevant territory (for example, one artist will be represented by only one gallery in Europe and potentially only one in the US), the divisions in design are not as easily stated. Due to the broad range of fields in which they work – from mass-manufacturing contracts with industrial producers to site-specific public installations, through retail and then to the gallery and auction milieu – designers have long learned to market themselves on a variety of different levels and to a number of different clients. For most, the gallery relationship is comparable to their relationships with other manufacturers or patrons, albeit far more personalised and intimate. Increasingly, though, some galleries are obtaining exclusive rights to a designer's primary-market work. It is not so much an issue of ownership but one of protection, for all parties. By being aware of the designer's output – where its going, how it's being handled and who it is being sold to – the gallery can help target it accordingly.

For the gallery, this protects their investment (both financial and emotional). For the collector, it helps guide them through the decision as to which galleries to make alliances with.

The reasons why one gallery chooses to work with a specific stable of designers over another are entirely informed by that gallery's specific agenda. Finances, geographical location and personal interest are all informing factors, however every gallery will state that the main determinant for a successful relationship is trust and respect. For a designer, the choices are similarly motivated by personal rationales, and often times fraught with anxiety as to if the gallery platform is even the appropriate platform for their work.

One major problem at the start of this, when I started talked about exclusivity to designers, was that they just froze. They thought, you're just trying to own me. Exclusivity actually doesn't mean that; it means protection and it means support, both financially and in terms of raising their provenance and their profile. And it ultimately allows you to have a real understanding of where their work is and being able to target a position.

Alasdhair Willis, director, Established & Sons, London[78]

I wasn't interested in working with galleries for a long time, as I hadn't come to my own conclusions about the system. Today, I think that this activity has a role to play and that it influences the rest of my work. Usually I don't have the latitude to be so radical.

Konstantin Grcic, designer, Munich[79]

By curating their exhibitions and in organising satellite events, such as talks, programmes and studio visits, and through publishing exhibition catalogues, monographs or catalogues raisonées, galleries have assumed some of the roles traditionally perceived as the preserve of the public institution. These added extras – as well as being good business practice – offer a layer of scholarly and financial value to the designer's works.

THE MAIN REASON WE
ENTERED
INTO THE GALLERY
'S
Y
S
T
E
M'
WAS TO BE ABLE TO
CARRY OUT RESEARCH AND TO
PRODUCE PIECES THAT WOULD
OTHERWISE NEVER HAVE BEEN
PRODUCED. WE TAKE MORE RISKS.
WE FEEL FREER,
INTELLECTUALLY SPEAKING,
TO MAKE MISTAKES.
DESPITE THIS RELATIVE
ABSENCE OF LIMITS,
THE WORK FOR THE GALLERY
ALSO INCLUDES CERTAIN RULES,
EVEN THOUGH
THEY CAN BE QUITE DIFFERENT
TO THOSE WE HAVE TO
RESPECT IN INDUSTRY.
WORKING WITH A GALLERY
IS LIKE BREATHING AGAIN.

As the production costs involved in design are often very high, there is a certain degree of pioneering spirit required for gallerists who are part entrepreneur/part patron. More often than not, the gallery allows the designer complete freedom from financial and technical constraints and, most importantly, allows time for these projects to mature, from first sketches to the presentation of the pieces. But the gallerist also offers business acumen, property and contacts to the designer as a type of research laboratory, so that designers can experiment and develop their ideas. Often the research carried out can be theoretical, meaning the pieces produced are not obliged to be functional or fully resolved.

[In 2000] only a very small number of editors were giving designers the scope to design particular pieces, and these were usually image pieces rather than mass-produced ones. In addition, marketing had started to take over to such an extent that designers had no freedom left. As a result, they needed a new system that enabled research: that of the gallery.

Clémence and Didier Krzentowski, Galerie Kreo, Paris [31]

Sometimes the gallery will take responsibility for manufacturing an object, working with the best craftsmen in various fields. The physical process of producing the edition past the initial prototype, while no longer the direct responsibility of the designer, is carried out to the designer's technical specifications. For example, much of Marc Newson's aluminium work is fabricated by a leading luxury-car manufacturer in the north of England, as only they have the tooling and capacity to create the highly polished and fluid forms his designs demand. In other cases, the responsibility for production is entirely that of the designer, though sometimes the gallerist is very rarely far behind them offering support and guidance.

This relationship also affects the financial arrangements between gallerists and designers. Percentages of profit are generally split between the two – the ratio differs from individual to individual, depending on the level of investment or the willingness of the dealer to take on the costs upfront. Works can also be brought into a gallery on a consignment agreement from either the designer or another gallery. Discounts are not mandatory. Gallerists might offer a discount (indeed, many build this into the pricing structure), but these are handled with discretion based on the original price, the buoyancy of the market, the rarity or uniqueness of the work and the level of commission the gallery earns from the sale. Larger discounts might be possible on the secondary market, as the dealer's investment in the work might be lower and the subsequent profit to be gained higher. Galleries can also offer purchase schemes – whereby the total purchase amount will be broken down into an agreed number of instalments over time. Again – this is at the gallery's discretion.

Galleries hold an important role, as a collector buys into the gallery's vision, trust and knowledge. Through the gallery's initial investment in the designer, the collector is also investing in the designer.

Ambra Medda, director, Design Miami/ [32]

SECONDARY MARKET

As heirs to the antiques trade, secondary-market dealers (and auction houses) offer a different kind of dialogue with their collectors and with the work they hold.

The secondary market acquires works from a number of sources, including auctions, private sales and other galleries. In a moribund market, the number of collectors de-accessioning (or selling) works from their collection can increase. Alongside the financial incentive, sometimes collectors will sell if the work is already represented in their collection by another example, or if they are fortunate enough to upgrade and therefore sell off any prior purchases.

If a collector is seeking a specific work from an earlier moment in a designer's career or works that the primary dealer cannot make available, secondary dealers might be the only route to securing a work. The relationship between the primary and secondary dealer can, however, be problematical, particularly if they are both dealing works by the one contemporary designer.

I think the churn is essential. If you have the capacity and the financial wherewithal to churn I think you have to accept there's a certain amount of churning that's going to happen as you stumble through your likes and dislikes and develop awareness and knowledge and visual finesse. And perhaps an attachment to a certain pedigree.

Michael Maharam, director, Maharam, New York [33]

If a collector chooses to buy the secondary market examples, it can have knock-on consequences for the primary market as it not only makes their investment and relationship with both the designer and the collector redundant but the prices at secondary market could be inflated, causing a shifting perception of that designer's market value.

Whether the collector's interest is in historic works or contemporary designs, the choice of which gallery to form allegiances and do business with is entirely dependent on personal motivation. There are many practical reasons that will inform this decision, be it subject-matter, approach, location or the personalities of the people involved. For new collectors wanting to research these (sometimes elusive) qualities, the advice would be to follow the art and design press for reviews and comments, talk (and listen!) to other collectors and use common sense as well as instinct.

There is often the lure of buying a piece from a gallery only to 'flip it' a couple of years later through auction or a secondary dealer, in the hope of making a profit. Such reselling of works so soon after purchase is taken as a slight by many galleries, for it suggests a lack of genuine interest in the work, and the provenance of that piece could be lost. It is an accepted courtesy that if a collector wishes to sell a work, they should do so through the original gallery (on either a consignment basis or outright, with the gallery purchasing the work from the collector). One reason for this is that the gallery can ensure the work goes to a suitable collection, sustaining its market value. The commission for this sort of arrangement is negotiable, depending on market values.

Some galleries make this mandatory, insisting on a signed 'resale agreement' before agreeing to sell the work for the first time. Other galleries take a more relaxed view, believing the owner has the right to do what they wish with their purchase. Either way, keeping the gallery informed of the intended future of an object will help inform the provenance of that piece, which is of benefit for designer, collector and dealer alike, and will preserve the relationship between the collector and the gallery. Buying works for purely speculative investment is a risky habit. It requires a certain amount of chutzpah, ample patience, a lot of crystal-ball-gazing and an infinite supply of financial resources to both acquire and maintain the works – yet it can yield very little by way of personal satisfactions or even monetary return. It's a gamble that many gallerists, dealers and seasoned collectors would not advise.

You do get the odd occasion where a buyer will surprise you and go for something completely different to their normal tastes. With the volatility of this market, I try to steer clear of the idea that the work is a great investment because it's dangerous to make those claims. I try to make sure that the buyer has a genuine attraction to the work and it is something they will enjoy.

Alasdhair Willis, director, Established & Sons, London [34]

CAVEAT EMPTOR

There are no real rules as to how transactions should or could happen. The gallery world is unregulated by any formal body, and therefore the individual is free to choose how they wish to operate – hopefully, honestly and openly. This does not preclude the collector from having their concerns or questions validated – they certainly should be made to feel confident and informed in their decision. Any uncertainties over price (including any associated taxes and duties), authenticity, date, dimensions, provenance, edition size, the condition of the work, the reliability or intended stability of the materials, and the installation or conservation requirements must be addressed and agreed to before the financial transaction is complete. Similarly, a collector should confirm insurance, delivery and installation details at the time of purchase – all of which are detailed in this book.

CONSULTANTS

Traditionally the preserve of interior designers, architects and decorators, the specific role of a design consultant and advisor is emerging as interest in collecting design grows. As their titles suggest, they offer a service to collectors in locating and securing works based on their knowledge of the international market. They also offer a support system for collectors who are not yet confident enough or wish to remain anonymous.

There has definitely been a rise in the field over the last five years for the hybrid expert – the person who's an architecture/interior design/collection adviser. But normally they would be specialists in a particular period: so they'd be focusing on 18th-century French and Continental furniture, for example. And then you have notable people working with 20th-century objects, whose output entirely revolves around 20th-century furniture. And you'd wonder why they'd never cross over, and that's probably because they weren't that comfortable dealing with both.

James Zemaitis, director of 20th-century design, Sotheby's, New York [35]

BUYING AT AUCTION

While the traditional auction house still exists, with its oak-panelled interiors, blue-chip work and the hushed tones of a pseudo-academia, the changing market and an influx of younger designers, buyers and sellers has had a knock-on effect, and most auction houses have now caught up with the 21st century. Some, like Phillips de Pury, have turned their salerooms into light open spaces where the atmosphere is more like a social gathering than a place of commerce. Of course, no one is pretending that sales aren't the *raison d'être* and bloodline of an auction house; however, such changes to the physical environment and attitude of the auctioneer or specialist have made the auction realm much more accessible and user-focused.

Dedicated design sales have been held at most of the international auction houses since the 1990s. The first was in London, at Bonhams in 1991, but the watershed moment occurred in New York, at Christie's East in November 1999, when the sale of some 135 lots tallied $1.8 million, an unprecedented figure. Like the obfuscation of terminology in the industry as a whole, how these sales are described is specific to each of the auction houses and has changed over recent years – from the 'applied and decorative arts' to 'design art' and then 'design'. They initially concentrated on vintage works or antiques from the 19th and 20th centuries. As these works became increasingly rare (coupled with a taste for more modern objects and a shifting market that appreciated design for its expressive quality), auction houses adapted accordingly.

Many have adopted the pre-sale strategies of the gallery market, demystifying the process of buying and curating the sale with stories and dialogues. By welcoming and drawing the collector into the process through their catalogues, pre-sale viewings and access to expertise, the auction house gives confidence and support to guide a collector's passion.

We are not just moving product and objects through the market-place. We don't just sit back and wait for objects to come in. Instead we proactively go out and search for the right pieces to curate a stimulating and considered sale.

Alexander Payne, worldwide director of design, Phillips de Pury, London [35]

In many ways, an auction house is a widely encompassing service – with a regular supply of high-quality objects and specialist expertise that can be passed on to a collector. The auction experience is, for the most part, a transparent and commercial process of supply and demand, with the work going to the highest bidder on the day. Despite the many reasons why a particular work might sell for certain sum, the fact that the price is in the public domain serves as an important, if not the only, public record of that designer's or object's market value.

As a result, many dealers and gallerists watch auction prices in order to respond accordingly, gathering information about who is bidding, on what, and for how much. They often bid themselves on works for clients or to add works to their secondary-market stock. The fact that an auction house is agreeing to sell a particular work is often a justification of that work's collectability. That there is someone willing to bid on the work offers peace of mind and increased confidence as well.

OPPORTUNITIES REALLY
SHOULD BE TAKEN
WHEREVER A COLLECTOR
FINDS THEM.
I HAVE CLIENTS
WHO SWEAR BY AUCTIONS,
AND OTHERS
WHO SWEAR THEM OFF.
THE REALITY IS THAT
THE BEST COLLECTIONS
ARE
BUILT BY
PURCHASING
WHEN THE
OPPORTUNITY IS RIGHT
- REGARDLESS OF THE
VENUE.

I think there is naivety on anyone's part – due to the speed with which information is disseminated – to think that the primary market and the auction market are not related in any way. The speed with which works can pass through markets has accelerated at such a rate. Because the public will decide on the market price of a piece at auction, and because auctions are so immediate, the auction house can benefit very quickly by benchmarking and exposing the designer in question to the marketplace. Also because it's now only really through an established gallerist or auction house that museums and collectors who missed out on the piece first time round have an opportunity to buy it.

Alexander Payne, worldwide director of design, Phillips de Pury, London [33]

For collectors new to auction procedures, it is useful to sign up to email updates with the auction houses, subscribe to catalogue services and research around the topic of your chosen interest. Perhaps the most important piece of advice is to strike up a relationship with the specialists in the auction house, as this will be a valuable route through the advantages and disadvantages of particular works and to the potential of a future collection.

All auction houses offer viewing periods, during which potential buyers can inspect and enquire after works. There is no charge to attend auction previews or to attend the actual auction. Whether or not the intention is to buy, attending the viewings and watching auction results (either in person or online after the sale) is essential for staying informed and learning about the vicissitudes of the market.

The Catalogue: Auction catalogues have, over recent years, become valuable assets to both the collector and auction house. No longer a staid publication of standard data, the catalogue is now a mini-encyclopedia of design history with exquisite photography. They are nearly as collectible as the objects represented within them. Richard Wright set the benchmark high at his eponymous Chicago auction house when, in 2000, he and his wife introduced beautifully designed, magazine-style catalogues. Alongside the relevant information about each of the lots (name, date, materials, condition, provenance and bibliography) many catalogues now include contextual forewords and essays. Most auction houses offer a catalogue subscription service, and many of the major houses present their catalogues online.

Pre-sale estimates are printed alongside each lot as a guide for prospective buyers. They are not, however, necessarily predictive of the final price or the potential value of the lot, and do not include the buyer's premium or taxes (see below). These estimates are reached from a number of sources, including the negotiations between the consignor and the auction house as well as the comparable value of other similar or identical works recently sold.

The reserve price is the confidential minimum price that the seller will accept. If there is no reserve price, this is normally indicated in the catalogue.

If we don't get details correct now, it will forever be in print until someone supersedes that catalogue. We have an obligation from both a contractual point of view and for the legacy of the piece. I see our catalogues as part of the legacy of the work. We are custodians of these works that will pass into future collections and generations, so we need to get the information right.

Alexander Payne, worldwide director of design, Phillips de Pury, London [89]

The Auction Preview: It is advisable to attend the auction preview, as there is no better way of judging the condition of an object than doing so in person. Experts should be on hand to answer any questions and to 'reveal' the object by helping turn, move or open it.

You can't tell the story of a piece by looking at the database of it. Catalogues go a long way, but people are starting to realise now that they have to handle everything, look at everything.

James Zemaitis, director of 20th-century design, Sotheby's, New York [90]

The Registration Process: Bidders will need to register and complete a bid form prior to auction in return for which they will be given some sort of bidder identification (normally a numbered paddle) to identify themselves during and after the auction. All bidders need to provide some form of identification, if not already held, to be kept in strict confidentiality by the auction house. This safeguards the auction house against defaults and fraud. Most auction websites provide very detailed guides to potential buyers and clearly outline their respective terms and conditions.

The Bidding Process: Bids can be made in several ways.

In person: being there to experience the atmosphere of the sale and the thrill of the chase is second to none, though the potential downsides are the loss of anonymity and the very real chance of going beyond a personal set limit in the heat of the moment.

By proxy: Having a representative bid on a collector's behalf offers a degree of anonymity, and can enhance a collector's bidding status and ultimate success.

Online: Live auctioneers will administer a collector's registration, process and execute all of their bids, and transfer any bids electronically during the sale.

Telephone: The collector will be called on the telephone during the sale, prior to the lot for which they have registered interest. The auction house's representative will relay the real-time bidding over the telephone and allow the collector to increase or decline the next bid accordingly. The actual conversation is brief and does not allow for much discussion. It is advisable to register a maximum bid in the event that the auction house is unable to reach the collector by telephone.

Absentee: If a collector is unable to attend an auction or bid by telephone, absentee bidding allows them to leave a written bid stating the maximum bid amount on an individual lot. During a sale, the auction house will bid on your behalf up to that amount. The written bid will only be seen by the auctioneer at the time of the auction, and only one absentee bid can be left per lot.

The auction is a transparent system. You have your catalogue and printed price, your auction day and paddle and if the work is worth how much you're willing to pay, it's as simple as that. That's why the thrill of the chase and the auction situation is so addictive and exciting.

Alexander Payne, worldwide director of design, Phillips de Pury, London [21]

Payment: Each auction house will have different requirements for payment procedures, outlined at the back of their catalogues. Buyers could be required to pay for purchases immediately following the auction, unless alternative arrangements have been made in advance.

Most auction houses charge the successful bidder a commission, or buyer's premium, on the hammer price of each lot sold. The buyer's premium is payable by the buyer as part of the total purchase price. The rates of this commission varies according to the value of the lot and the auction house, but can be 25 percent of the hammer price up to and including £25,000, 20 percent of the portion of the hammer price above £25,000 up to and including £500,000, and 12 percent of the portion of the hammer price above £500,000.

Value added tax may be payable on the hammer price and/or the buyer's premium, depending on whether or not the work has been imported from outside the EU and is to be exported outside the EU. In the US, state taxes may apply. Consult the terms and conditions in the catalogues.

For online bidding, an additional charge can be incurred. Again, consult the guides at the back of each catalogue for confirmation. Once paid, a certain amount of storage time is offered free, after which the item must be collected or incur storage charges. Insurance on the works, extra packaging and transport are normally the responsibility of the purchaser; however, the auction house should be able to advise on reputable companies to oversee transport and shipping logistics.

The biggest difference in recent years has been the volume in the marketplace. Based on the demand, volume has increased 100-fold. One need only add up the pre-sale estimates of the design sales in December 1999 and compare them to the December 2009 presale estimates to see the enormous increase of material entering into the marketplace.

Peter Loughrey, director, Los Angeles Modern Auctions[92]

DESIGN FAIRS

Traditionally a design fair was an industry-only event where manufacturers promoted new designs and the latest developments purely to the industry. But just as the nature of design evolved in tandem with consumers' increasingly sophisticated interest, so too did these fairs. Most of the formerly trade-only events now have a schedule of publicly accessible presentations. London Design Festival, Milan Furniture Fair (Salone del Mobile) and New York's International Contemporary Furniture Fair (ICFF) are three of the main contenders, yet a host of cities and countries present their own 'design weeks' with talks, events, exhibitions and displays of contemporary design. For a collector, these are an exciting and affable source to tap for information about young talent, established names and major developments in materials, processes and concepts – all of which affect the development of the contemporary collecting market.

When an entire city celebrates design, like Milan does during Salone del Mobile, it can only reinforce that design has vibrancy and importance.

Ambra Medda, director, Design Miami/[93]

It all changed again in December 2002 when the seed of an idea was hatched in Miami to coincide with Art Basel Miami Beach – the sister event to Art Basel, the leading international art fair for collectors. From the initial 2002 party called 'Art Loves Design', it metamorphosed into a series of exhibitions, talks and events to become a fully fledged fair in its own right by 2005. Design Miami/ grew out of the professional and personal interests of Craig Robins, a design collector, art patron and the developer of Miami's Design District. Robins, the fair's director, Ambra

IT'S
OK TO
BUY SOLELY
FOR INVESTMENT
BUT THAT WILL USUALLY
SET COMPLETELY DIFFERENT
PARAMETERS THAN THOSE OF A
COLLECTOR WHO SIMPLY WANTS TO
DECO-
RATE
THEIR
PRIMARY
RESIDENCE
OR SOMEONE WHO
WANTS TO DECORATE
A VACATION HOME. ADVICE
FOR BEGINNING COLLECTORS
NEEDS TO BE TAILORED TO THEIR
REASON FOR ENTERING THE MARKET.

Medda, and the then director of Art Basel, Samuel Keller, took the lessons from Basel and established a sister event to coincide with the art fair in June. By piggy-backing on to the art fair, Design Miami/ and Design Miami/Basel capitalised on an existing audience of museum directors, curators, critics, collectors, dealers and journalists, all of whom had come both for the fairs and the social encounters. In fact, the relationship to Art Basel is more than just piggy-backing, as Messe Schweiz, the parent company of Art Basel, is an equal partner in the Design Miami/Basel show, and a minority shareholder in the worldwide rights.

Antiques dealers have long associations with the more conventional collector-orientated fairs (think Grosvenor House Antique fair), however Design Miami/ offered the first design-specific fair for (predominantly) 20th- and 21st-century design. For the organisers, it had many catalysts: the increased interest from galleries, dealers and the designers themselves; a generation of collectors eager to ensure their physical surroundings were comparable with their art collections; and the organisers' personal agenda of drawing attention to the value of design. Robins has been open about the positive mutual benefits of the development of Design Miami/ and of the Design District (where the fair has been held every December since launching).

By its second year, Design Miami/ had proven itself beyond all expectations. At the time Medda was quoted as saying, 'Initially I was just hoping the dealers would sell enough to pay for their booths and transportation, but sales have been incredible.' During Design Miami/'s inaugural showcase, an Yves Béhar chandelier sold for $434,600 and a Pierre Szekely screen was reportedly bought by Donna Karan for $350,000.

Design Miami/ was a targeted effort to make the statement – which until that point no one had made to that level – that design was collectible. It has been an amazing opportunity to learn about design, to meet the most important dealers in the world, to see historical material in the context of contemporary material. It took it out of this notion of the antique fair and made it feel very much part of the moment.

Craig Robins, CEO Dacra, co-founder Design Miami/[25]

These satellite design fairs represented a physical coupling of design and art that obviously mirrored the coupling in the minds of both gallerists and collectors.

Mayer Rus, design editor, *LA Times* [25]

Design fairs are made up of galleries and dealers presenting their stable of works, though their density and frenetic pace offer a considerably different collecting experience to that of the gallery and should not be overlooked. The design-specific fairs (and those, such as FIAC and Pavilion of Art & Design, that include a mix of fine art, sculpture and design) offer an unprecedented platform for encountering every type of design in a single space, from antiquarian treasures, through Modernist masters to contemporary works. They also provide an unparalleled chance for collectors to meet many of the key players in the field, as most of these people – who are often inaccessible in a gallery environment – will be present, whether participating or not. Most fairs have strict vetting policies, to ensure the quality and reliability of both the galleries and the designs on show. Authenticity is an important part of this vetting process; some galleries have had to remove items from their fair booths if they cannot validate these works or if they do not meet the strict and connoisseurial high standards.

The key to visiting the fairs is obtaining one of the various levels of VIP pass (not all VIPs are equal; they are ranked on a sliding scale of privilege and timed access). The fair organisers, sponsors, galleries and dealers invite their clients to these VIP previews and sometimes museum-patron groups also gain early access. Without that golden ticket, whatever its hue, there is a very real chance that the collector will find the best deals will have already been made before the fair opens to general admission. However, this is not always the case – it takes a keen eye and a lateral appreciation of what might be considered 'key'.

Alongside the overtly commercial activities, many of thefairs curate a series of cultural programmes, such as satellite exhibitions, performances and talks that explore the issues surrounding contemporary design practice and collecting. Of course there are also the social lures of attending, with

Maarten Baas, designer, Den Bosch[99]

EXHIBITIONS IN MIAMI + BASEL ARE THE KEY MOMENTS TO PRESENT NEW WORKS. IT'S AMAZING HOW IMPORTANT THEY BECAME FOR THE WHOLE DESIGN WORLD AND SPECIFICALLY THE LIMITED-EDITION DESIGN WORLD– MAYBE MORE IMPORTANT THAN MILAN.

like-minded collectors, passionate dealers and galleries, acres of museum-quality design and the thrill of the chase in the air. There is a lot to be said of this frenzied and collective atmosphere, as it helps bring intrigue and interest to collecting which, if channelled correctly, helps sustain the market.

Each gallery or dealer will have their own way of handling potential transactions. As a general rule, however, when purchasing a work from a fair it is important to make sure the sale is definite and all details of price, payment strategy, gallery contacts, transport (including delivery date) and shipping insurance are confirmed, or at least acknowledged as needing further discussion, before walking away from the fair.

Fairs are obviously more democratic, or more democratic-feeling environments. They're less threatening. They're more like shops, I suppose, than museums or galleries. And everyone knows how to behave in a shop. Everyone knows what you're there for.

Matthew Slotover, director, Frieze, London[23]

I grew up with art, but the designs that I grew up with are much less contemporary, so the fairs have been wonderful in bringing design to people's doorsteps. It is very difficult to navigate your way through the design world because there is so much out there and there are no historical references apart from those which are very decorator- or movement-specific.

Yana Peel, co-founder, Outset, London[22]

MUSEUMS AND PATRONAGE

It is impossible to overstate the importance of museums in giving legitimacy to design connoisseurship. Among many others, London's Victoria & Albert Museum and Design Museum, New York's MoMA and Museum of Arts and Design, the Art Institute of Chicago, the Vitra Design Museum in Weil am Rhein, the Pompidou Centre in Paris and Boijmans van Beuningen Museum in Rotterdam have all contributed to the increasing collection, display, education and promotion of design appreciation.

These institutions (which, while independent from commercial pressure, are not completely free from market constraints or critique) offer a critical exploration of collecting habits and the many technical, material and conceptual developments from a wide historical span.

Funding and support for new museums of design (Design Museum, Holon) and the rehousing of existing museums (New York's Museum of Art and Design and the Design Museum in London) are adding to the international awareness of design's collectability and value as a socio-economic, political and cultural indicator. As new museums open and existing museums review their design collections, the challenge is to identify the unique reasoning behind why and what they collect. It would make little sense for MoMA, the V&A and the Centre Pompidou all to be presenting the same objects from the same designers – not something that art galleries necessarily need concern themselves with.

It is important to understand the role institutions play in setting standards of collecting, scholarship and conservation and, appropriately, value. Exhibitions of major periods of design history and figures of both historical and contemporary interest help set an agenda for the collecting market while also helping establish and further the reputations of the designers involved. The academic kudos afforded by such institutional acknowledgement is priceless, and the savvy collector would be well advised to keep abreast of museum programming internationally.

For furniture we (led by Christopher Wilke) were very interested in design innovation as a key factor of the object we were considering for acquisition; did it change something in the way things were done? Did it lead? Or was the designer a leader? Maybe a certain shape or form is adopted later and becomes a style, or it could be an early development of a technique or a particular way of working for a particular market sector. Those are all things that you can apply very easily to product design, industrial design, and I think Christopher's thinking was around expanding the design for production collections rather than the one-offs and the craft pieces. It's slightly different when you're looking at craft objects because innovation hasn't been a key driver. It's conservation, or conservatism, rather, that's the driving force.

Gareth Williams, Senior Tutor of Design Products
at the Royal College of Art, formerly Curator of 20th-century
and contemporary furniture at the V&A, London [101]

When we're looking for work for the museum, we're not looking for acts of perfection; we're looking for acts of invention, works that show a pivotal moment in a designer's body of work, a shift in their practice where they've been able to innovate, or design that suggests new ways of making, new materials. Really it's design that speaks about the time in which it was made and is very much a social, historical commentary. I'm constantly thinking, will this piece have value for us in a hundred years? What will it tell us about how we are living today?

Zoë Ryan, Neville Bryan Curator of Design, Art Institute of Chicago [102]

Design is very much like a story. You don't have to own a story for it to give you something; you just need to hear it – to allow it to be communicated. Although we need people to buy our work and it's fantastic when they do, purchasing the work is not essential for the work to fulfil its narrative function – to tell the story, to have questions asked of it. That can happen in a museum, on the pages of a magazine, through an exhibition, not just through ownership. It's one riposte to the criticism that this type of design is elitist.

Julia Lohmann & Gero Grundmann, designers, London [103]

PATRONAGE

Becoming involved with an internationally recognised institution enhances the integrity and perceived value of the individual's collection, as it suggests that the collector is informed, interested and connected.

From its earliest beginnings, the relationship between public museums and private collectors has been a close and often mutually beneficial one. While these relationships may not always be as celebrated as the bequests endowed by 19th-century fine-art patrons, they have helped museums establish and maintain high standards of curatorial and collecting policy, while offering the benefactor the prestige and peace of mind that comes from a bequest being conserved for future generations.

Patronage schemes are of bilateral benefit: they offer a sliding scale of access to the benefactor (relevant to the financial support given) and important income to the museum. It is a rare institution that can exist without financial support from its patrons. While some museums operate exclusive invitation-only membership, all museums have a tiered membership scheme open to anyone willing to join, regardless of their location or available time to participate in the more user-centred benefits of membership. The categories within each scheme range from the basic 'friends' donation through to platinum-level patronage. While curators and museum directors are appropriately protective of their curatorial and collecting agendas, it is an unstated fact that the more a collector gives, the greater the access to the inner workings of the institution.

A selection of patronage schemes and educational facilities is offered at the end of the book.

We're very privileged to be able to live with these things, but for me it's the opportunity to show it to a broader audience. And it's exciting for me to see it in a curated show among other works, and how it's been incorporated.

Michael Smith, collector, London [104]

DONATING WORKS

While institutions rely on the generosity of their patrons and of collectors, not everything that is offered can be accepted. A responsible acquisitions policy will question if the resources required to conserve and preserve a donated object are available, if the work is of sufficient value (historically, technically, thematically) to fill a gap in the collection, and if the object is in sound condition. However, with the spiralling costs of contemporary design, few museums have an acquisition budget that will allow them to develop their collection without help – be it donations in money or in kind.

As with art, collectors can benefit financially by bequeathing works to certain museums, although obviously this is entirely dependent on the tax laws of the relevant country.

OTHER SOURCES

Retailers: One-off, autonomous and collectible design is not necessarily the preserve of galleries and dealers. A select handful of progressive retailers were championing unique and small-volume design objects long before some galleries were in existence. That they do so in an environment with which most consumers and collectors feel familiar can make the process seem less threatening (or less exclusive) than buying through a gallery. The best of these expose the public to innovative design and new concepts, ranging from industrial design by established brands to handcraft and individual makers – illustrating how the two can site together comfortably.

Murray Moss, owner of what the *New York Times* in 2003 called 'arguably the best design store in America', has said, 'We can show and sell "experiments" that may be in too early a stage to be seen on a larger level, but still need to be seen. I don't represent a balanced picture of the design landscape. I could end up with a store full of blue objects made by German women. That's why the store is called Moss. It's about what resonates with me.'[105]

I want to show that design is not just about aesthetics or conceptual appreciation, but that it could and should be invited straight into the heart of family life precisely in order to enrich the quality of lifestyle. Essentially I wanted to make design, and the enjoyment of it, as accessible as possible. While galleries do go far in showcasing new ideas, they often fail to make the ideas accessible to the general public, and this is the main aim of Mint.

Lina Kanafani, Mint, London [103]

Commissions: Commissioning new designs – site-specific installations or more speculative objects – is a rewarding form of patronage. The negotiations go beyond any regular bill of sale, as the relationship between commissioner and designer obviously involves a significant amount of discussion, understanding, trust and patience before the design process starts. While miscommunication and misguided expectations are par for the course, the benefits of commissioning should outweigh any negatives.

Some would argue that the point in commissioning should be to have something unique in concept and realisation, not simply to modify an existing contemporary design to suit the practical requirements of the collector. However, as pragmatists, most designers will respond to the brief and work with the collector to meet any specific requirements.

Issues to bear in mind:

- An understanding of the designer's work is crucial to getting the best results out of the individual

- There should be a clear brief that states the collector's parameters and boundaries

- Have a budget and a realistic time frame – though be prepared to be flexible

- Depending on the relationship a designer has with a gallery, the negotiations might need to be put through the gallery

- Get confirmation – or at least acknowledgement – from the designer as to the rights and licences of the work, and particularly if they intend to develop the ideas in the commission into an edition at a later date, and any corresponding documentation to help safeguard the commission if the designer should choose to do so

What I like about the table we commissioned from Martino Gamper is that he made it with us in mind. It's changed our relationship of sitting and eating in ways I didn't quite expect. We obviously liked it, we commissioned it, but we didn't really expect how it would come into and affect our life.

Emily King, design historian, London [107]

I always said that to do something good you need four or five elements. One is courage, another is vision. Third is a good accountant and a lawyer, and you need money. So money you can get: you have it or you get it from a bank or a sponsor or whatever if you have an interesting idea. The lawyer and accountant, you can ask your friends who is the best one and fit to the system you need, so it's not a big deal. Courage… Vision you can buy from an art director, an artist, a designer and so on. But courage, if you don't have the courage to put the vision in action, it doesn't matter how much money you have and how good your accountant is.

Arik Levy, designer, Paris [108]

You have to be very confident in your own taste and in the work you're commissioning, because things can change along the route between the idea and what you actually get. Despite all the nightmares: the delays, the money upfront, the fact that you don't really know what you're getting, I feel that part of me is in the objects.

Janice Blackburn, curator, London [109]

Knowing the elements and the requests of the commissioner, I can play and produce within these requirements. Within those kinds of constraints, anything can happen.

Maarten Baas, designer, Den Bosch [110]

Direct from designer: Long before there was a mainstream, there were designer-makers or artisans who chose to create and develop their designs on a small scale. Today there are numerous contemporary designer-makers who welcome visitors to their workshops – akin to artist's studio visits – to view their design and production processes. Not all are completely divorced from industrial design, nor is every designer working in autonomous and studio-based design affiliated with a dealer or gallery, but their work lies somewhere in between, like an update of the pre-industrial relationship between arts and crafts.

Accessing information and contact details through online searches and trade fairs is a relatively easy and lucid process. Most designers have websites and use fairs such as the Milan Furniture Fair, London Design Festival and New York's International Contemporary Furniture Fair (ICFF) as a platform for their work. Without a gallery involved, there are no related dealer fees – but this does not necessarily mean the work will be a bargain. In producing high-quality, small-volume works without the support network of a gallery or industry to offset the expenses, the designer's raw costs (material and production) could be high, and these will be passed on to the collector. Rarely would a designer sell the work at cost, so a collector should anticipate paying for the concept (akin to buying a licence for the object), as well as the time, energy and expertise that has gone into its production.

The great joy of dealing with the contemporary is you've got the people there. For the moment, at least, design isn't so baroque … the design world isn't so complex and you still have access. Contemporary art might be more difficult, as there are lots of gate-keepers, but even if there is an agent or gallerist involved with the designer, it still seems that you can get to the source much more easily.

Gareth Williams, Senior Tutor of Design Products
at the Royal College of Art, formerly Curator of 20th-century
and contemporary furniture at the V&A, London

Degree shows: Increasingly, postgraduate and graduate designers are seizing opportunities during their degree shows to sell their final collections direct to dealers and collectors (as opposed to the convention of marketing new works to manufacturers). It is undoubtedly rewarding to support designers early in their career, and degree shows offer the perfect platform

Matthew Hilton, designer, London 112

I THINK WE
HAVE
A
NATURAL
CONNECTION TO
THINGS MADE BY HAND.
PEOPLE TALK OF THE
'INDIVIDUALITY'
AND
'IMPERFECTIONS'
THAT MARK OBJECTS
AND MAKE THEM SPECIAL,
BUT THE DIFFERENCE BETWEEN
SOMETHING WHICH HAS THESE
MARKS OF INDIVIDUALITY
AND OF MAKING AND
IS
BEAUTIFUL
BECAUSE OF THEM,
VERSUS SOMETHING NEARING
THOSE MARKS AND JUST BEING
BADLY MADE, IS VERY, VERY
SUBTLE.

for talent-spotting. The pitfall is that the high costs of producing prototypes and realising designs, coupled with concurrent economic restraints on colleges for staff technicians, tooling and machinery, mean that some of these works remain at prototype stage and should be bought in full awareness of any limitations inherent in the object. Not all colleges or graduate designers are struggling. Certain governments, aware of the importance of design education and graduate funding, offer support systems and financial grants to emerging design practices.

In the Netherlands, for example, arts-academy graduates are entitled to funding for the first four years of their professional practice and can apply for additional subsidies to assist in their living and working costs. Ultimately this has lead to a market swell of well-educated, well-financed and well-equipped designers, and is largely responsible for the increasing number of Dutch graduate designers in the collector's market.

The quality of a college is also informed by the quality of its tutors and department heads. As this is in continual flux, it is worth keeping abreast of the changes.

Since 2009 alone Tord Boontje has replaced Ron Arad as professor and head of design products at London's Royal College of Art; Jurgen Bey has moved from the Royal College to be the director of the Sandberg Institute in Amsterdam; Lidewij Edelkoort retired from her post as chairwoman of the Eindhoven Design Academy in 2008 – Anne Mieke Eggenkamp now holds the post, but the school still seeks a creative director after Alexander Van Slobbe left abruptly in 2009; Gareth Williams transferred from head of 20th-century and contemporary furniture at the Victoria and Albert Museum to senior tutor of design products at the RCA in 2009; Pierre Keller is due to retire as director of the École Cantonale d'Art de Lausanne; Paul Thompson recently replaced Christopher Frayling as rector and vice-provost of the RCA, leaving his former post of director of the Cooper-Hewitt in New York; Mark Breitenberg took over from long-time president Stephen Beal as provost at the California College of the Arts in 2009; the Parsons in New York underwent several faculty changes in 2009, including William Morrish moving from the University of Virginia to become dean of the School of Constructed Environments, and the school appointed Miodrag Mitrasinovic as dean of the School of Design Strategies.

Understanding these nuances, as well as the track record of certain colleges to produce quality students, is vital to being at the right college at the right time to discover new talent.

Another pitfall is that, as the market for emerging design grows, so too do the number of dealers and gallerists competing for access to emerging designers' work. Knowing the calendar of degree shows – and associated platforms, such as London's annual New Designers or the college exhibitions at events such as Milan's Salone del Mobile – will furnish the collector with as much chance as discovering new talent as the gallerist. There are no real rules of engagement in collecting from degree shows. Given the propensity for design to be produced in editions (be they small or large), the designer is under no formal obligation to the collector and could continue to sell later editions of the work. It is worth discussing this with the designer and obtaining documentation from them as to the nature of their purchase.

Internet: Many online art indexes now have specific areas devoted to 20th- and 21st-century design. These are valuable tools for plotting a designer's market value, but using the internet for confirming factual information should be approached with caution, as it is obviously not a regulated system.

Most auction houses preview their catalogues online, list post-sale results and offer auction alerts to assist collectors in planning their calendar. Gallery websites are used as marketing and promotional tools for the works they represent.

The wave of websites selling design online continues to swell. From the obvious sites such as eBay through to more sophisticated and reputable search-engine-orientated portals such as DeTnk and 1stDibs, the proliferation of websites selling design online escalates daily. So too does the potential to make expensive or frustrating errors of judgement. As a general rule, collectors should exercise caution with authenticity, condition and the quality of transportation when purchasing collectible design over the internet.

LOGISTICS

First and foremost, the purchasing collector should confirm who is responsible for organising and paying for the safe delivery of their work. If it is the collector's responsibility, auction houses, galleries and dealers will often recommend reputable companies. It is good practice to obtain several estimates prior to committing to a company.

The method and grade of packing and shipping will be chosen to suit the length and type of journey, and the peculiarities of the work in question. Many insurers will not cover loss or damage to works damaged in transit unless they have been packed and shipped by professional fine-art shippers.

Local galleries and museums, cultural attachés or embassies, and recognised bodies such as the International Convention of Exhibition and Fine Art Transporters (ICEFAT) can also supply recommendations and advice. It is important to remember that regulations are constantly being updated and new ones added. A responsible agent should be aware of all the current regulations and be able to advise accordingly.

PACKING

Different objects require different methods of packing, which should be resolved as soon as an art handler or method of transportation has been chosen.

If the dealer has not already arranged to do so, the shipping company should be requested to professionally pack the items in conservation-quality materials.

Bubble wrap – while cheap and readily available – should be used with extreme caution. It should never be wrapped directly around the surface of the object, as the gases given off from the plastic could leave bubble marks on the surface, which are near-impossible to remove. Instead, use an interlayer of acid-free tissue paper or some other conservation-quality material before applying the bubble wrap with the bubbles facing away from, rather against, the surface. Like many plastics, bubble wrap deteriorates over long periods of time, especially when exposed to inappropriate environments.

Ensure that there are no loose items or sections inside a crate that could jostle around and potentially damage other objects. Though bespoke crates can often be expensive, and the responsibility of storing or disposing of crates lies with the collector, they are often the safest way to transport goods. If transporting internationally, the crates should conform to international regulations. Due to recent embargos on untreated timber, all timber packaging must meet the IPPC's international standard for a phytosanitary measure and its guidelines for regulating wooden packaging material in international trade (known as ISPM15). Each wooden package must show a special stamp to indicate that it is ISPM15-compliant. Crates should be secured with screws, not nails, so as to avoid potential risk to works during unpacking.

If you are reusing packing material, make sure that it is clean and free of mould, mildew or debris. It may be worth the investment to purchase new, clean materials for each move.

TRANSPORT

It is advisable that the transport company be a member of recognised international freight organisations, such as:

- British International Freight Association (BIFA)
- American Moving and Storage Association (AMSA)
- European Freight Forwarders Association (EFFA)

Issues to consider when choosing the transport company include:

- Ask for credentials and qualifications, and keep a note of contact details for further communications about the task, particularly while the shipment is en route.
- How will the item be packed – will it be crated or wrapped?
- Will packaging be commercial, semi-museum or museum grade?
- How many people are on the crew, and will this be sufficient to load and unload the goods?
- How are environmental concerns, such as temperature and humidity, regulated on long journeys?
- What security and tracking precautions does the company employ, both en route and at points of pickup and delivery?
- Will the vehicle be unattended for any portion of the trip? If so, how will the vehicle and its contents be guarded?
- Does the company have security and airside clearance at the airport?
- Will the unloading of a shipping container be supervised?
- Is there any compensation or costs for delay?

Not all of these issues will be relevant or necessary, but by asking detailed questions of the company, the collector will not only be offered peace of mind but also impress upon the shipper their serious intent and expectations of service. Once the company has been chosen, the handler will need to know:

- the artist or designer's name
- the title or description of the object
- the size, which should include all three dimensions, indicating which dimension is the height – this should be the largest of the three
- the medium, or what it is made of
- its fragility
- does the object dismantle into several components? If so, how?
- its age
- the value of the object
- the agent will also need confirmation on packing so they can accommodate for this throughout the item's journey.

The customs status of the object is important, too. The handling agent might need to know if the object has been sold 'tax free' for export from the vendor's country, if the work is under a special customs regime, e.g. customs 'bonded' warehousing, temporary admission/import. The vendor should advise information on this at point of purchase as it can affect what can be done and how the object is moved.

Modes of Transport: Despite what may initially seem an easy choice, the method of shipment should be carefully considered as it could have an impact on the wellbeing and timely arrival of the work, regardless of how well it is packed and reputable the shipper. The shipper will be able to recommend the best option for the work, and will base this recommendation upon budget, size, weight, fragility of the item and the optimum delivery deadline.

Often the size can rule out various transport options or routings. Likewise, the weight has a bearing on how the object can be moved and handled, and whether any special equipment may be required. It's important to remember that regulations are constantly changing, being updated, or new ones added. A reputable fine-art handling agent would be aware of all the current regulations and able to advise accordingly.

Air: Objects must always be properly cased for air freight. The size and weight of the packed case will dictate which aircraft the case will fit on and therefore the available routings. Quite often, it is not possible to fly direct and the case needs to be shipped via a central hub airport. In some cases it may not be possible to fly direct, or to fly at all, depending on the size and weight of the object, and the size of the aircraft.

For particularly fragile and valuable objects it is possible – with the correct security access passes – for the fine-art handling agent to supervise the loading and unloading of the aircraft cargo units inside the cargo shed, and if required the loading and unloading of the cargo units to and from the aircraft on the tarmac. This supervision process ensures the safe handling of the packed case by the airline's handlers and further minimises risk.

Recent security regulations stipulate that every item travelling by air must be hand-searched, X-rayed or compression tested for explosive devices. In such cases, specialist agents must declare each shipment has been searched and certify its safety according to international standards. Lists of such agents can generally be found on the appropriate country's governmental websites.

For air freight, there are special aviation security regulations that must always be adhered to. These vary from country to country, usually with several different methods of certifying the shipment as safe to travel by air freight, according to the circumstances. Local handling agents would be able to advise about the most appropriate method for any particular shipment.

Road: Road transport is often the most cost-effective, but not necessarily the fastest. At times, road is the only option for national or continental journeys, where aircraft are too small or are not unitised. Road transport should be by air-ride vehicles as these have the smoothest ride and the least vibration, which can damage the objects. Ideally vehicles should be temperature or climate-controlled as changes in temperature or humidity have a detrimental effect on objects.

Provided the objects are moved on specialist fine-art vehicles, it is not always necessary to case them. Objects could be moved soft-wrapped, as they will always be moved and handled by trained fine-art handling technicians.

A further cost-effective option for road freight is a part-load. This is where a fine-art handling agent is able to offer space on a vehicle for a number of suitable and compatible shipments, splitting the overall costs between the various shipments. Collectors cannot choose when the objects are to move; instead, the object has to move when the handling agent's vehicle is going. Schedules are given so the collector can decide whether the timing works for their particular shipment or not. The usual analogy is that a part-load shipment is like a bus, whereas a dedicated shipment is like a taxi. General road haulage, while a more economical option, is really only suitable for transporting items for that do not require specialist handling.

Sea: Sea freight is mostly used for intercontinental shipments. Overall journey time is considerably longer than air freight, with vessels likely to be leaving on a weekly rather than daily basis. The two options are full container load (FCL), in which a 20- to 40-foot container is used solely for the shipment of your goods, and groupage (LCL). The latter, a shared-container option, is more cost effective than FCL shipping, as costs are divided by the amount of shipments travelling in the same container. While this option is cheaper, it is nevertheless worthwhile asking for an FCL quote when the shipment is in excess of 15 cubic metres.

Environmental conditions for the objects are much more changeable for sea freight than by other modes of transport, and it is therefore not considered a good option for vulnerable objects that are particularly susceptible to big changes in environmental conditions. If containers or vessels are not loaded correctly, there is a risk of objects moving around inside the container, and in extreme conditions it is possible that containers can go overboard and be lost at sea. [114]

Tax Issues: A customs entry is a legal declaration. It is therefore important that all information provided is correct and accurate. Customs officers do make inspections and audits of exporters, importers and fine-art handling agents; any discrepancies or errors may not be picked up by customs for several years, but at that point they will want it put right.

Detailed information on the objects is required to allow for their accurate classification within the customs tariff, as this is the basis for duty and tax rates. Incorrectly classifying objects, particularly in attempt to gain lower duty and tax charges, is unacceptable to customs.

In most countries there is no customs duty on artwork or antiques. This can extend to other collectibles, although they may be subject to duty depending on the particular nature of the object, its country of origin and the laws of the importing country. Note that customs duty is different to excise duty; excise duty relates to alcohol, hydrocarbon oil and tobacco products.

Most countries have some sort of sales tax, such as VAT, TVA or GST. Many countries also have a special reduced tax rate for artwork and antiques, which again can extend to other collectibles depending on the nature of the object (e.g. the UK has a special reduced VAT rate of 5 percent for the importation of artworks). It should also be remembered that private individuals must still declare objects imported and pay the appropriate duty and tax, even if it is for their own use.

When buying goods, it is usually possible to 'avoid' paying the tax in the buying country, provided the object is exported correctly and the correct customs export documentation is provided to the seller. Usually the seller will assist in the export arrangements. Sometimes the seller may ask for the tax to be initially paid; it will then be refunded once the correct customs export documentation has been received.

It is always important to find out the customs status of the object, so that the necessary formalities can be attended to and the correct documentation produced. Failure to make correct and accurate customs documentation can result in fines from the relevant authorities, usually as a percentage of the object value. For customs purposes, the whole of the European Union is effectively considered as one big country, so purchases from other EU countries are usually (but not always) in free circulation. Free circulation means that all applicable duties and taxes have been paid in one of the EU countries; they will not need to be paid again in another EU country, and can freely move within the EU without further customs documentation or intervention. However, this does not remove the need for export licences or permits when the need arises.

Many shipping companies offer special customs clearance services, and can advise on the matter, but always check with the appropriate government agency for specific requirements.

It should be the responsibility of the shipping company to arrange clearance and prepare any documentation, such as ATA carnets (also called a 'merchandise passport', this international customs document is issued and recognised by 70 countries, and is presented when entering a country for items that will be re-exported within 12 months). However, the collector should nevertheless confirm any licensing or tax ramifications for which they might be liable.

Taxes and duties vary widely according to country, and so should be discussed at length with the shipping company and researched prior to shipment.

Licences: Understanding regulations in both the country of origin and destination is important, and advice can be sought through the gallery or auction house, handling agent or through bodies such as Unesco, which provides a database of worldwide cultural legislation.

Exporting Licence: Many countries have cultural goods export licensing regulations which require an export licence for any object that breeches certain age and value thresholds. Regulations and thresholds change so you should refer to the local art handling agent for specific information at the time of shipment.

Objects which contain parts of endangered animal or plant species (e.g. ivory, tortoiseshell, mahogany) require CITES licensing (Convention on International Trade in Endangered Species). Such licences are required from both the exporting country and the importing country for any shipment. Regulations are particularly onerous, and it usually takes several months to get the correct licences. Some countries also restrict which ports the objects can arrive at, so that a specialist government agency is on hand to make the appropriate checks (e.g. imports into the United States must be through designated US fish and wildlife ports).

DELIVERY AND INSTALLATION

Good communication is key. It is essential to provide the handlers with access details, including information about street parking, access to the property (including any steps and landings) and if machinery or specialist tools are required to lift the crate or object. An obvious point to stress is to ensure that the works can be received at their destination – make sure there is a responsible party to oversee the safe delivery and unpacking and that either that the crate or the object can physically fit into the property. Once inside, there should be adequate room for the crate or object to be manoeuvred into position.

The collector should advise the handler in advance if they want assistance in unpacking the object, disposing of the empty packaging, and installing the object. Ultimately the crate is the responsibility of the collector to store or dispose of, but most handlers can assist in these matters.

Once unpacked, inspect the object thoroughly for signs of a change in condition or previously undetected faults before signing any paperwork. A signature constitutes the owner's approval of the object's condition and all liability is transferred to the owner. If in doubt, a conservator or representative of the gallery should be on site to oversee the proceedings.

Most furniture purchases do not require specialist installation attention. For electrical items or works that are suspended from fittings or fixtures, seek the advice of a professional. Depending on the nature of the work, this could require extensive preparation (reinforcement, wiring, additional fixings) and a preliminary site visit from a professional is advised. Request advice from the gallery or auction house if needed.

DISPLAY CONDITIONS [115]

Caring for collections also involves controlling the environment in which the items are placed. Inorganic materials, such as ceramic, stone and metals, tend to be fairly robust, though silver will tarnish in polluted atmospheres. Wood, textiles and paper all respond to moisture, and therefore the collector should avoid extremes

in temperature and humidity. In hot, dry conditions, wood may warp and crack, whilst in moist conditions it will swell. Keeping the conditions stable is therefore important to long-term preservation. Avoid placing items directly above a radiator or in a humid bathroom. Dust and dirt disfigure items and damage can occur whilst cleaning.

Light causes irreversible damage, either by fading dyes in textiles or by causing photochemical degradation of the material itself. Some plastic will darken and become brittle over time and silk will 'shatter', i.e. lose all its strength. Natural light contains ultraviolet light, which will accelerate damage. In museums, films are placed on all windows to filter out the UV. In a private collection this may not be possible, so avoid placing any light-sensitive materials in direct sunlight or in front of a window. Avoid using spotlights on the items, or limit the illumination to when the objects are being viewed. Turn lights off at night and store smaller items in drawers or boxes to reduce light damage. [115]

Wash hands thoroughly and wear gloves before handling any metal objects, as the chemicals in the skin are transferred onto the metal surface and cause corrosion. The imprint of the fingers becomes etched into the surface layers of the metal and the metal will have to be polished to remove them.

Avoid using any wet materials if a dry surface brushing will suffice. Use pure products rather than commercial cleaning products, as these often include perfumes, water softeners or bleaches that can all cause either immediate damage or problems in the longer term if they are not fully removed. For example, gently wiping a solid surface (like a metal or glazed ceramic) with a dry, soft cloth or brush is adequate in removing dust. Pure tap water with a few drops of pure soap (such as non-perfumed baby products) will remove dirt, but the surface will need to be rinsed.

For anything more than a surface clean, contact a conservator.

STORAGE

Whether the collector uses a professional fine-art storage company, a private storage unit or chooses to store items at home, there are certain issues to bear in mind:

- The environment should be dry, temperature-controlled and preferably climate-controlled to maintain consistent conditions.
- Adequate security systems should be installed.
- Fireproofing and/or alarms should be in place.
- All works within storage should be clearly labelled for ease of identification and access.
- Handling can be one of the most damaging actions that an item can undergo. Support the item whilst it is moved, avoid picking it up by the handle (which is often the weakest point) and place items in boxes or baskets with padding around them to transport them between locations.
- For long-term storage, ensure materials used are as inert as possible. Use acid-free or archival-quality padding and boxing. Organic materials such as textiles, fur and feathers, leather and skin can be a food source for insects and rodents. Check the items regularly (twice a year) for signs of insect infestation.

Professional storage: Many fine-art handling agents provide suitable storage facilities to their clients, both within open-plan warehouses and as individual storage units, but there are also companies just providing fine-art storage facilities.

Conditions a collector should insist upon are:

- 24hr CCTV cameras and an approved alarm and intruder system

- smoke and heat sensors throughout
- climate control to maintain consistent conditions
- tracking procedures for tracking and recording the movement of objects and crates
- experts on hand to advise on longer-term conservation and storage issues
- in the UK only, government indemnity to insure the warehouse meets governmental standards

Some facilities also offer serviced storage, including goods receiving, photographic inventories, viewing spaces, checking, repacking and delivery – however, this will incur considerable extra costs. Storage charges are usually based on the volume of the packed work, or the overall volume of the space. In some instances, charges are based on the floor area that the object takes up. Usually insurance companies will have knowledge of the fine-art storage companies and may be able to offer an opinion on the suitability of a warehouse.

I have a marvellous lady who I've never met, who's been looking after my artworks now for over five years. I have telephone conversations with her, email conversations with her. Every so often she sends me a bill. And she has been invaluable. I've never seen how much I have. I see through an inventory, but I have never physically seen it, and I think it might freak me out.

Michael Smith, collector, London [117]

INSURANCE [118]

While in the gallery, institution or auction house, an object will usually be insured under their cover. As soon it leaves these premises, it becomes the buyer's property and is thus the collector's responsibility to insure. Transit insurance must be considered and put into place before the object moves anywhere.

Many shipping companies have trading conditions that will limit their liability in the event of any damage, so clarifying this liability is important.

Specialist art insurance brokers should be able to offer transit coverage within an existing insurance policy, which is much more economical than buying a specific policy for the transport of individual pieces. Worldwide coverage is available for collectors who regularly buy abroad.

For design works kept in the home, household and contents insurance is an economical option; however, some insurance companies will refuse to cover valuable works or simply be ill-equipped to understand the value of certain design works.

Additionally the collector might find they have restricted cover, very high premiums and, worst of all, a claim being inadequately settled or in the worst case rejected. It is advisable to seek the advice and services of a specialist art insurance broker.

Specialist insurers like to insure art. This is because collectors take great care of their works, and so the claims ratio is usually low. Therefore, specialist insurers always offer the most competitive premiums. Indeed premiums have never been as low as they are at present. Economies of scale also come into play, so it is generally cost-effective to insure a collection as part of a household policy. Again, specialist household policies will include a specific section on art and design collections, and the insurers will employ experienced art-claims handlers. A good broker will also be able to recommend ways to reduce premiums whilst maximising cover; this will include recommending higher excesses.

A specialist 'private collector' policy addresses every insurance requirement for a collector. Adequate cover in a policy should generally provide the following:
- items insured on an agreed-value basis
- all risks as standard (i.e. everything is covered except what is specifically excluded)
- cover for loss in value/depreciation following a claim for accidental damage is automatically included
- worldwide cover is automatically included
- transit is automatically included
- new items automatically covered at point of purchase (this is called the 'acquisitions clause')
- items automatically covered when for sale at auctions
- ability to extend cover and issue the relevant documentation if works are lent to museum or galleries

There are very few exclusions under a specialist policy, but a common exclusion is the process clause, which means that there is no cover for items damaged while being repaired, restored, retouched or any similar process. Similarly there is no coverage for loss or damage caused by wear and tear, gradual deterioration, inherent defect, rust or oxidation, moths or vermin, warping or shrinkage – all of which are important factors for design collectors to bear in mind if the objects form part of their household furnishings. Other standard exclusions include loss, war, radiation and radioactivity, while the threat of terrorism is an issue to be discussed directly with the broker.

If an object is damaged and cannot be restored, then the option of declaring the piece a 'total loss' will be available. Indeed, some insurers allow the collector to declare a total loss even if the damage is minimal. This would mean insurers pay the agreed value of the work to the collector and then would take ownership of the damaged work. All claims costs, such as restoration, transit and storage, will be covered by the policy. Many insurers will not cover loss or damage to works damaged in transit that have not been packed and shipped by professional fine art shippers. It is worth noting that some collectors chose to insure design items for the refabrication costs only, which can save premiums as these costs are usually considerably less than the market value. Generally, brokers only advise this action if the collector is absolutely certain the artist/designer will refabricate works.

The issue of valuations can be tricky. Again, a specialist insurer will normally take the view that a collector will know the value of works in their collection and so will not insist on independent professional valuations, which can be expensive. Dealers are able to advise on current prices and a professional valuation can then be undertaken approximately every three to five years, which allows the benefit of constant cataloguing of all items in a collection.

A good valuation should include the following details:
- Type of object
- Materials and techniques
- Measurements
- Inscriptions and markings
- Distinguishing features
- Subject
- Title
- Date or period
- Maker

However, what matters most is that the values of items to be insured are agreed upon beforehand, to avoid any disagreement in the event of a claim. It is recommended that collectors maintain schedules of their collection with insurance values and that these records are updated at renewal each year.

CONSERVATION AND RESTORATION [119]

Preserving and conserving acquisitions requires ongoing care and attention to detail; paints can fade, plastics can discolour and organic materials are susceptible to all environmental conditions.

I don't think that conservation should become a litmus test to whether you collect an item or not. I think you've just got to be very responsible and open-minded. Otherwise, you wouldn't buy anything from Joseph Beuys, for example. You wouldn't buy any sort of video art from the 1970s.

Zoë Ryan, Neville Bryan Curator of Design,
Art Institute of Chicago [120]

Asking the designer, gallery or auction house about the (sometimes intended) future of the work can be a valuable means of ensuring a plan of action should issues arise. Being informed is the most valuable tool, as often ill-informed decisions and bad advice can lead to detrimental and irreversible damage.

Should an item require conservation, or should anything go wrong, there are steps the collector can take to intervene. Damage should be addressed as soon as possible, and professional advice and services sought immediately. Most museums and institutions have a conservation department that accepts public enquiries, but contacting the dealer or gallery could yield more immediate results.

Specialist groups, including the Institute of Conservation (ICON), the International Institute for Conservation of Historic and Artistic Works (IIC) and the American Institute for Conservation of Historic and Artistic Works (AIC), can also be contacted for advice and recommendations. Most of these bodies have information about care of collections on their websites and run a conservation register, which will put the independent collector in contact with conservators in their locality who have the appropriate expertise to treat their collections.

Increasingly, museums and heritage organisations publish information on their websites regarding collections care. The Victoria and Albert Museum has an extensive range of material on care of different materials and conservation. It includes the *V&A Conservation Journal*, which is now published annually and reflects the care and treatment of V&A-based collections from archaeological material to contemporary furniture, fashion and flat art. It also investigates the care of plastics, theatre and performance collections and toys.

There are also a number of publications available, but perhaps the most reputable and pragmatic is *The National Trust Manual of Housekeeping: The Care of Collections in Historic Houses Open to the Public* (Oxford: Elsevier Butterworth Heinemann, 2006). It is interesting to note that in their sale catalogues, Phillips de Pury include the following disclaimer:

'All lots with electrical and/or mechanical features are sold on the basis of their decorative value only and should not be assumed to be operative. It is essential that, prior to any intended use, the electrical system is verified and approved by a qualified electrician. All items of furniture in auction sales are either items not originally supplied for use in a private dwelling or are offered for sale as works of art. The items may not comply with the Furniture and Furnishings (Fire) (Safety) Regulations 1988 (as amended in 1989 and 1993) and for this reason should not be used in a private home.' [121]

One example of the importance of controlling the temperature occurred in a recent exhibition where a vase made of honeycomb, borrowed from a private gallery, was on display during one of the warmest summers that the museum had experienced for several years. The possibilities of using fans and refrigeration systems in the showcase were explored, but ultimately we had to have staff on call ready to take the vase off display and place it in a cool room should temperatures be reached where the wax would begin to deform and melt. Luckily, the vase survived without damage.

Sandra Smith, head of conservation,
Victoria and Albert Museum, London [122]

Restoration: The collector should be aware of the designer's intent, as it is entirely possible that a conservator's advice might alter original elements and, therefore, an item's integrity.

Reconstruction, strengthening, and re-sewing require an understanding of the materials from which the object is made and how they were originally constructed. If the wrong materials are used, or are applied in an inappropriate manner, then the item can be damaged irreversibly and it will cost considerably more for a conservator to intervene.

With Deco you have to look very carefully at condition, authenticity and provenance. You need to come at it like you're buying a vintage car: Who drove it, who owned it, how much restoration and tampering has been done, does it have the right doors and engine and transmission? And then with some mid-century pieces, patina and original finishes – that's an especially tricky area.

Adam Lindemann, author and collector, New York [123]

It's very much driven by the culture that surrounds the particular micro-market. For example, in French Art Deco, when you're dealing with six-figure works by Ruhlmann, there is a long-established tradition of these pieces being kept in perfect condition at all times. It doesn't have a major impact on the value of the piece. On the flipside, when you are dealing with historic works of Modernism where the only reason a person would be interested in the chair in the first place is because it's from the very first series of work by that designer or the workshop, then original condition becomes everything. And so a Rietveld 'Zig Zag' chair that has been refinished at a later date becomes a huge doubter compared to one that's in it's original shape with its original paint.

James Zemaitis, director of 20th-century design, Sotheby's [124]

APPENDICES

ANNUAL EVENTS

JUNE

Degree Shows

École cantonale d'art de Lausanne (ÉCAL)
Lausanne, Switzerland, www.ecal.ch
Umeå University, Umeå Institute of Design
Umeå, Sweden, www.dh.umu.se
The Glasgow School of Art
Glasgow, Scotland, www.gsa.ac.uk
Central St. Martins College of Art & Design
London, www.csm.arts.ac.uk
Royal College of Art
London, www.rca.ac.uk
Chelsea College of Art and Design
London, www.chelsea.arts.ac.uk
University of Art and Design
Helsinki, Finland, www.uiah.fi
School of Design, The Hong Kong Polytechnic University
Hong Kong, www.sd.polyu.edu.hk

Design Festivals and Fairs

DMY Berlin International Design Festival, www.dmy-berlin.com
A contemporary design forum founded in 2003 that exposes emerging talent, established designers and developments in contemporary design. Open to the public.
Design Miami/Basel, www.designmiami.com/basel
Founded in 2004, Design Miami/Basel, along with its sister event Design Miami/, assimilates international dealers, designers, curators, collectors and critics. The fair promotes general interest in design and elevates appreciation for limited-edition, experimental and historically significant design work. Open to the public.

JULY

Degree Shows

Central St. Martins College of Art & Design
London, www.csm.arts.ac.uk
Royal College of Art, London
www.rca.ac.uk
Chelsea College of Art and Design, London
www.chelsea.arts.ac.uk

Design Festivals

New Designers, London, www.newdesigners.com
New Designers presents cross-disciplinary works by over 3000 graduates from architecture to animation and fashion to furniture. Open to the public.
SOFA (The International Expositions of Sculpture Objects & Functional Art), Santa Fe, New Mexico, www.sofaexpo.com
International galleries and dealers present works that bridge the worlds of design, decorative and fine arts, with an acclaimed lecture series and educational special exhibits. Open to the public.
Design Tokyo, www.designtokyo.jp
Trade fair and industry affiliates only.
Sydney Design, www.sydneydesign.com.au
In its 14th year, this event encourages debate about the confluences of contemporary life and design. Most events open to the public.

AUGUST

Design Festivals

Copenhagen Design Week, www.copenhagendesignweek.dk
Seeks to raise awareness of contemporary Danish designers, attracting design experts, tourists, students and international media to prominent design-related activities. Most events open to the public.

SEPTEMBER

Design Festivals and Fairs

Maison & Objet, Paris, www.maison-objet.com
This annual tradeshow targets professionals from the field of interior design. Trade fair/industry affiliates only.
London Design Festival, www.londondesignfestival.com
Assembles individuals and organisations from across the design spectrum for a week-long event. Open studios, product launches, trade shows, major international exhibitions, private views and site-specific public installations take place. Most events open to the public.
100% Design, London, www.100percentdesign.co.uk
Attracts international manufacturers, designers and industry figures from the worlds of architecture and design and promotes contemporary interior products. Trade fair/industry affiliates only.
Tent London, www.tentlondon.co.uk
This annual event takes place in the Truman Brewery, a former industrial site, as part of the London Design Festival. Industry affiliates and general public welcome.

OCTOBER

Degree Shows

Eindhoven Design Academy
The Netherlands, www.designacademy.nl

Design Festivals and Fairs

Prague Design Days/Designblok, www.designblok.cz
Annual exhibition which takes place in selected showrooms, boutiques and galleries. A programme of talks, award presentations and an introduction of designers and design studios to manufacturers accompanies the event. Most events open to the public.
Pavilion of Art and Design, London, www.padlondon.net
Formerly known as DesignArt London, and a sister event to PAD Paris and PAD New York, this fair highlights fine and decorative arts and design of the 20th and 21st centuries, and is timed to coincide with Frieze Art Fair. Open to the public.
The Midcentury Show, Bristol, www.modernshows.com
Highlights furniture and collectibles from the mid-20th century. Open to the public.
FIAC (Foire d'art contemporain), Paris, www.fiac.com
A meeting place for international collectors and industry buyers, FIAC promotes contemporary fine and decorative art. Exhibitions of emerging artists, outdoor installations and performance art pieces accompany the event. Most events open to the public.
Dutch Design Week, Eindhoven, www.dutchdesignweek.nl
Takes place in over 60 locations, featuring Dutch design through exhibitions, lectures, workshops and company visits. Most events open to the public.
Origin, London, www.craftscouncil.org.uk
An opportunity to buy directly from nearly 300 contemporary craft makers, with work ranging from functional tableware to knitwear, jewellery and millinery. Interactive events and late-night viewings

attract industry insiders and general audiences alike.
Open to the public.
Vienna Design Week, www.viennadesignweek.at
Promotes the fields of product, furniture and industrial design,
while positioning experimental design as a central tenet.
In cooperation with Viennese museums, design studios and
production and retail companies, the city hosts themed exhibitions,
venue-specific installations, discussion events and a programme
of films. Most events open to the public.

NOVEMBER

Design Festivals and Fairs

100% Design Tokyo, www.100percentdesign.jp
Launched in 2005, 100% Design Tokyo (an offshoot of 100%
Design London) is a trade show for contemporary Japanese
designers and interior design companies. Trade fair/industry
affiliates only.
100% Design Shanghai, www.100percentdesign.com.cn
Like its sister events in London and Tokyo, this trade show offers
contemporary interior design products including furniture, lighting
and home accessories. Trade fair/industry affiliates only.
Singapore Design Festival, www.singaporedesignfestival.com
Curated selections and events reflect the progression of
Singaporean designers. Most events open to the public.
*SOFA (The International Expositions of Sculpture Objects & Functional
Art), Chicago, www.sofaexpo.com*
International galleries and dealers present works that bridge the
worlds of design, decorative and fine arts. Also features
an acclaimed lecture series and educational special exhibits.
Open to the public.

DECEMBER

Design Festivals and Fairs

Design Miami/, www.designmiami.com
Launched in 2005, Design Miami/, along with its sister event Design
Miami/Basel, assimilates international dealers, designers, curators,
collectors and critics. The fair promotes general interest in design
and elevates appreciation for limited-editioned experimental design
work. Open to the public.

JANUARY

Design Festivals and Fairs

Art Palm Beach, www.artpalmbeach.com
International contemporary art, photography and design.
A range of satellite events, installations and community outreach
programmes accompany the festival. Open to the public.
The Passagen, Cologne, www.voggenreiter.com
Exhibitors include institutions and museums, such as Museum
Ludwig and the Museum of Applied Art, Cologne, alongside
universities, studios, showrooms, galleries, furniture stores and
international manufacturers. Open to the public.
Maison & Objet, Paris, www.maison-objet.com
This annual tradeshow targets professionals from the field of interior
design. Trade fair/industry affiliates only.
*IMM Cologne (The International Furnishing Show)
www.imm-cologne.com*
Trade show exhibiting home interiors. Trade fair/industry
affiliates only.
Experimenta, Lisbon, www.experimentadesign.pt
ExperimentaDesign Lisboa/Amsterdam is a cultural biennale

dedicated to design, architecture and contemporary creativity.
The event generates and showcases original projects, concepts
and ideas in different formats including conferences, screenings,
exhibitions, urban interventions, workshops and debates.

FEBRUARY

Design Festivals and Fairs

Experimenta, Amsterdam, www.experimentadesign.pt
As above.
Palm Springs Modernism, www.modernismweek.com
20th-century decorative and fine arts. Coincides with Palm Springs'
annual Modernism Week, a celebration of modern design and
architecture. Events include film screenings, lectures and gallery
openings. Open to the public.
Object Rotterdam, www.objectrotterdam.nl
Focuses on current developments within the international design
field. The fair is a platform for unique and limited-edition functional
design objects, crafts and jewellery. Open to the public.
Design Indaba, Cape Town, www.designindaba.com
Design Indaba highlights advertising, film, music, fashion, graphic
and industrial design, architecture, craft, new media and visual
and performing arts. In addition to conferences and expositions,
Design Indaba also presents publications, educational events
and community initiatives. Most events open to the public.
Stockholm Design Week, www.stockholmdesignweek.com
Stockholm Design Week is a citywide programme of commercial,
cultural and alternative exhibitions. Showrooms, museums,
galleries, retail outlets and furniture stores garner public attention
with special exhibits, seminars and events. Most events open to
the public.

MARCH

Design Festivals and Fairs

TEFAF Maastricht, www.tefaf.com
This fine art and antiques fair showcases more than 250
international dealers. Open to the public.
Le Pavillion des Arts et au Design Paris (PAD Paris), www.padparis.net
Like its sister events in London and New York, PAD Paris highlights
fine and decorative arts and design of the 20th and 21st centuries.
Open to the public.
Midcentury.Modern, London, www.modernshows.com
Dealers offer Scandinavian, European and American mid-century
furniture and decorative arts, as well as contemporary wallpaper,
ceramics, accessories and gifts. Open to the public.

APRIL

Design Festivals and Fairs

*Salone Internazionale del Mobile (Milan Furniture Fair/Milan Design
Week), www.cosmit.it*
This international trade show highlights the best of the home
furnishings sector. Besides commercial offerings, the Salone
Internazionale del Mobile also provides a host of educational events
for both industry and the general public alike. Trade fair/industry
affiliates only (many events open to the public)
*SOFA (The International Expositions of Sculpture Objects & Functional
Art), New York, www.sofaexpo.com*
International galleries and dealers present works that bridge the
worlds of design, decorative and fine arts. Open to the public.

Art Fair Tokyo, www.artfairtokyo.com
Contemporary and modern art and antiques. Open to the public.
Luminale—The Lighting Culture Biennale, Frankfurt
www.luminapolis.com
Lighting design. A platform for architects, designers and artists
to exhibit their latest work to international trade visitors and the
general public. Satellite events, lighting projects and installations
take place around the city.

MAY

Degree Shows

Rhode Island School of Design
Providence, www.risd.edu
Parsons the New School for Design
New York, www.parsons.edu
Savannah School of Art and Design
Georgia, www.scad.edu
York Sheridan University, Department of Design
Toronto, http://design.yorku.ca/
University of California Los Angeles (UCLA), Department
of Design & Media Arts
Los Angeles, www.design.ucla.edu
University College of Arts, Crafts & Design (Konstfack)
Stockholm, www.konstfack.se
École nationale supérieure de création industrielle
Les Ateliers, Paris, www.ensci.com
Politecnico di Milano, Facolta di design
Milan, www.design.polimi.it
State Academy of Art and Design Stuttgart
Stuttgart, www.abk-stuttgart.de
Tama Art University
Tokyo, www.tamabi.ac.jp
Köln International School of Design
Cologne, www.kisd.de
The Academy of Arts & Design, Tsinghua University
Beijing, www.ad.tsinghua.edu.cn
Design Akademie Berlin
www.design-akademie-berlin.de

Design Festivals and Fairs

Collect: The International Art Fair for Contemporary Objects
London, www.craftscouncil.org.uk
Annual international fair for collectible ceramic, glass, silver,
jewellery, metalwork and more made by established creatives
and emerging talent. Open to the public.
Los Angeles Modernism, www.dolphinfairs.com/lamodernism
International 20th-century decorative art and furniture.
Open to the pubic.
ICFF (International Contemporary Furniture Fair), New York
www.icff.com
Interior designers, architects, retailers, manufacturers, distributors
and developers all exhibit at this showcase for contemporary design.
ICFF also provides a considered programme of supplementary
events. Trade fair/industry affiliates only.

PATRON SCHEMES

Victoria & Albert Museum Director's Circle
www.vam.ac.uk/support_us/patrons/index.html
For more information, contact membership@vam.ac.uk
Design Museum Membership Schemes
designmuseum.org/membership
For more information, contact development@designmuseum.org.
Museum of Modern Art (MoMA) Membership Schemes
www.moma.org/support/membership/index
For more information, contact membership@moma.org.
Museum of Art & Design (MAD) Membership Schemes
madmuseum.org/GET_INVOLVED/membership.aspx
For more information, contact patrons@madmuseum.org.
The Museum of Contemporary Art, Los Angeles (MoCA)
Membership Schemes / *www.moca.org/museum/join_home.php*
For more information, contact membership1@moca.org.
The Art Institute of Chicago Membership
www.artic.edu/aic/joinaic/membership.php
www.artic.edu/aic/members_donors/support/index.html
Centre Pompidou, the Société des Amis du Musée
(The Friends of the Arts Décoratifs)
www.centrepompidou.fr
For more information, contact amis.mnam@centrepompidou.fr or
lesamis@lesartsdecoratifs.fr.
Museum Boijmans Van Beuningen Individual Partner Scheme
& The Friends of Museum Boijmans Van Beuningen
www.boijmans.nl/en/ For more information, contact info@boijmans.nl
MUDE Lisbon (Museo do Design e da Moda)
www.mude.pt/en / For more information, contact mude@cm-lisboa.pt.
Cooper-Hewitt, National Design Museum Membership
cooperhewitt.org/SUPPORT/membership.asp
For more information, contact chmembership@si.edu.
MAK Art Society (MARS), Vienna (Austrian Museum of Applied
Arts and Contemporary Art)
www.mak.at/e/service/f_service_mars.htm
For more information, contact MAKartsociety@MAK.at.
The National Museum of Art, Architecture and Design, Oslo
Sponsorship Programme
www.nationalmuseum.no/index.php/content/view/full/1537
For more information, contact info@nasjonalmuseet.no.
The Montreal Museum of Fine Arts Support Schemes
www.mbam.qc.ca/en/amis/amis_seulment.html
www.mbam.qc.ca/en/financement/cercle_du_president.html
For more information, contact membership@mbamtl.org
Museum of Design Atlanta Member Schemes
www.museumofdesign.org
Design Museum Helsinki, Friends of the Museum Scheme (DAMY)
www.designmuseum.fi
Design Museum Holon
www.dmh.org.il / For more information, contact friends@dmh.org.il
Vitra Design Museum
www.design-museum.de
For more information, contact communications@design-museum.de
La Triennale di Milano Design Museum
www.triennaledesignmuseum.it
For more information, contact tfriends@triennale.it
Design Museum Gent
design.museum.gent.be/ENG
To support the Design Museum Gent, contact museum.design@gent.be.

NOTES

WHY (pp. 9–25)

1 Bruce Chatwin, *Utz* (London: Penguin, 1988), p. 20.

2 Walter Benjamin, *Illuminations*, trans. H Zohn (London: Jonathan Cape, 1970), pp. 61–62.

3 Susan Pearce, *On Collecting* (Oxon: Routledge, 1995).

4 Matthew Slotover, director, Frieze, London. In conversation with the author, February 2010.

5 Murray Moss, Moss, New York. In conversation with the author, February 2010.

6 Marcel Brient, collector, Paris. In interview with Christian Simenc, Galerie Kreo, *Sixteen New Pieces* exhibition catalogue, 2008.

7–8 Jean Baudrillard, *The System of Objects*, trans. James Benedict (London: Verso, 1996), p.85.

9 Philippe Starck, designer, Paris. In conversation with the author. August 2003.

10 Mark Rappolt, editor, *Art Review*. In conversation with the author, February 2010.

11 Michael Maharam, director, Maharam, New York. In conversation with the author, February 2010.

12 Reed Krakoff, collector, New York. Quoted in *Art + Auction*, April 2007. Article by Julie Iovine, p. 124.

13 Mayer Rus, design editor, *LA Times*. In conversation with the author, February 2010.

14 David Gill, David Gill Galleries, London. In conversation with the author, February 2010.

15 Mark Rappolt, editor, *Art Review*. In conversation with the author, February 2010.

16 Ambra Medda, director, Design Miami/. In conversation with the author, January 2010.

17 Yana Peel, co-founder, Outset, London. In conversation with the author, February 2010.

18 Michael Maharam, director, Maharam, New York. In conversation with the author, February 2010.

19 George Lindemann, collector, Miami. In conversation with the author, February 2010.

MODERNIST GOALS? (pp. 27–35)

20 Tom Dixon, designer, London. In conversation with the author, February 2010.

21 Jean-Pierre Camard, quoted in 'A tour of Eileen Gray's hideaway', by Lara Marlowe. *Irish Times*, 6 July 2009.

22 James Zemaitis, director of 20th-century design, Sotheby's. In conversation with the author, March 2010.

23 Gareth Williams, Senior Tutor of Design Products at the RCA, formerly Curator of 20th-century and contemporary furniture at the V&A, London. In conversation with the author, February 2010.

24 George Nelson, 'The Design Process at Herman Miller'. *Design Quarterly*, 1975, pp. 6–9.

WHAT (pp. 37–57)

25 Steve Jobs, founder and CEO, Apple, Cupertino, California. Quoted in 'One-dollar-a-year man', *Fortune* magazine, 24 January 2000.

26 Erik Adigard, communication designer, Sausalito, California. Quoted in 'A conversation about the good, the bad and the ugly', moderated by Chee Pearlman, *Wired* magazine, January 2001.

27 Julia Lohmann, designer, London. In conversation with the author, February 2010.

28 Zoë Ryan, Neville Bryan Curator of Design, Art Institute of Chicago. In conversation with the author, February 2010.

29 Dieter Rams, designer, Kronberg, Germany.

30 Paola Antonelli, Senior Curator, Department of Architecture and Design, Museum of Modern Art, New York. Quoted in 'A conversation about the good, the bad and the ugly', moderated by Chee Pearlman, *Wired* magazine, January 2001.

31 Generic term for a member of the Bauhaus school, originally founded in Germany by Walter Gropius in 1919.

32 Tom Dixon, designer, London. In conversation with the author, February 2010.

33 Didier Krzentowski, director, Galerie Kreo, Paris. In conversation with the author, January 2010.

34 Tom Dixon, designer, London. Quoted in Sophie Lovell, *Limited Edition* (Basel: Birkhäuser, 2009), p. 118.

35 Tony Chambers, editor-in-chief, *Wallpaper**. In conversation with the author, February 2010.

36 Pierre Keller, director, ECAL, Lausanne. In conversation with the author, February 2010.

37 James Zemaitis, director of 20th-century design, Sotheby's. Quoted in lecture *Collecting Design: What Are the Strategies of Major Collectors and How Do the Art and Design Markets Relate?*, Design Miami/, December 2007.

38 Mayer Rus, design editor, *LA Times*. In conversation with the author, February 2010.

39 Jurgen Bey, designer, Rotterdam. Quoted in Sophie Lovell, *Limited Edition* (Basel: Birkhäuser, 2009), p. 120.

40 Alice Rawsthorn, design critic, *International Herald Tribune*. In conversation with the author, February 2010.

41 Alasdhair Willis, director, Established & Sons, London. Quoted in *Icon* Issue 52, October 2007.

42 Gareth Williams, Senior Tutor of Design Products at the RCA, formerly Curator of 20th-century and contemporary furniture at the V&A. In conversation with the author, February 2010.

43 James Zemaitis, director of 20th-century design, Sotheby's. Quoted in lecture *Collecting Design: What Are the Strategies of Major Collectors and How Do the Art and Design Markets Relate?*, Design Miami/, December 2007.

44 Barry Friedman, Friedman Benda Gallery, New York. Quoted in *Icon* Issue 52, October 2007.

MANUFACTURED VERSUS UNIQUE (pp. 59–69)

45 Higher Education Statistics Agency, 2005.

46 Casper Vissers, co-founder, Moooi, Amsterdam. In conversation with the author, March 2010.

47 Lina Kanafani, Mint, London. In correspondence with the author, March 2010.

48–9   Maarten Baas, designer, Den Bosch.
In conversation with the author, February 2010.

50   Casper Vissers, co-founder, Moooi, Amsterdam.
In conversation with the author, March 2010.

51   Maarten Baas, designer, Den Bosch.
In conversation with the author, February 2010.

52–3   Murray Moss, Moss, New York.
In conversation with the author, February 2010.

54   Penny Sparke, *The Genius of Design* (London:
Quadrille Publishing. 2009), p. 235.

55   Maarten Baas, designer, Den Bosch.
In conversation with the author, February 2010.

CONTEMPORARY THEMES (pp. 85–147)

56   Alice Rawsthorn, design critic, *International Herald
Tribune*. In conversation with the author,
February 2010.

57   Arik Levy, designer, Paris. In conversation with the
author, February 2010.

58   Nigel Coates, 'Street Signs', in John Thackera (ed.),
Design After Modernism (Thames & Hudson, 1988),
p. 109.

59   Jurgen Bey, designer, Rotterdam. Quoted in Sophie
Lovell, *Limited Edition* (Basel: Birkhäuser, 2009), p. 120.

60   Marcus Fairs. Quoted in Design Miami/Basel
catalogue 2007.

61   Sarah van Gameran, designer, Studio Glithero,
London. Quoted in correspondence with the author,
March 2010.

62   Ambra Medda, director, Design Miami/.
In conversation with author, January 2010.

63   Tomáš Gabzdil Libertiny, designer, Rotterdam.
In correspondence with the author, March 2010.

64   Zoë Ryan, Neville Bryan Curator of Design, Art
Institute of Chicago. In conversation with the author,
February 2010.

65   Arik Levy, designer, Paris. In conversation with the
author, November 2009.

66   Gaetano Pesce, quoted in 'Ugly' by William Wiles,
Icon Issue 61, July 2008.

67   Bertjan Pot, designer, Rotterdam. Quoted on his
website, www.bertjanpot.nl.

68   Gareth Williams, quoted in 'Ronan and Erwan
Bouroullec', by Alice Rawsthorn. *International Herald
Tribune*, 20 January 2008.

EXTERNAL INFLUENCES (pp. 149–155)

69   *Time* magazine, April 2005.

70   Alice Rawsthorn, *Marc Newson* (London: Booth-
Clibborn Editions, 1999), p. 8.

71   Marc Newson, designer. In conversation with the
author, March 2009.

72   Alice Rawsthorn, design critic, *International Herald
Tribune*. In conversation with the author, February 2010.

73   Alexander Payne, worldwide director of design, Phillips
de Pury. Press release, May 2009.

74   Marcel Brient, collector, Paris. In interview with
Christian Simenc, Galerie Kreo, *Sixteen New Pieces*
exhibition catalogue, 2008.

HOW (pp. 157–195)

75   Zoë Ryan, Neville Bryan Curator of Design, Art
Institute of Chicago. In conversation with the author,
February 2010.

76   Ben Evans, director, London Design Festival.
In conversation with the author, February 2010.

77   Brian Kish, dealer, New York. In conversation with the
author, February 2010.

78   Alasdhair Willis, director, Established & Sons, London
In conversation with the author, January 2010.

79   Konstantin Grcic, designer, Munich. In interview with
Christian Simenc, Galerie Kreo, *Sixteen New Pieces*
exhibition catalogue, 2008.

80   Ronan Bouroullec, designer, Paris. In interview with
Christian Simenc, Galerie Kreo, *Sixteen New Pieces*
exhibition catalogue, 2008.

81   Clémence and Didier Krzentowski, Galerie Kreo, Paris.
In interview with Christian Simenc, Galerie Kreo,
Sixteen New Pieces exhibition catalogue, 2008.

82   Ambra Medda, director, Design Miami/.
In conversation with the author, January 2010.

83   Michael Maharam, director, Maharam, New York.
In conversation with the author, February 2010.

84   Alasdhair Willis, director, Established & Sons, London.
Quoted in *Icon* Issue 52, October 2007.

85   James Zemaitis, director of 20th-century design,
Sotheby's. In conversation with author, March 2010.

86   Alexander Payne, worldwide director of design, Phillips
de Pury. In conversation with the author, January 2010.

87   Peter Loughrey, director, Los Angeles Modern Auctions
(LAMA). In email correspondence with the author,
February 2010.

88–9   Alexander Payne, worldwide director of design, Phillips
de Pury. In conversation with the author, March 2008.

90   James Zemaitis, director of 20th-century design,
Sotheby's. In conversation with the author, March 2010.

91   Alexander Payne, worldwide director of design, Phillips
de Pury. In conversation with the author, January 2010.

92   Peter Loughrey, director, Los Angeles Modern Auctions
(LAMA). In email correspondence with the author,
February 2010.

93   Ambra Medda, director, Design Miami/.
In conversation with the author, January 2010.

94   Peter Loughrey, director, Los Angeles Modern Auctions
(LAMA). In email correspondence with the author,
February 2010.

95   Craig Robins, CEO Dacra, co-founder Design Miami/.
In conversation with the author, March 2010.

96   Mayer Rus, design editor, *LA Times*. In conversation
with the author, February 2010.

97   Maarten Baas, designer, Den Bosch. In conversation
with the author, February 2010.

98   Matthew Slotover, director, Frieze, London.
In conversation with the author, February 2010.

99   Yana Peel, co-founder, Outset, London. In conversation
with the author, February 2010.

100   Tony Chambers, editor in chief, *Wallpaper**.
In conversation with the author, February 2010.

101   Gareth Williams, Senior Tutor of Design Products
at the RCA, formerly Curator of 20th-century and
contemporary furniture at the V&A, London.
In conversation with the author, February 2010.

102	Zoë Ryan, Neville Bryan Curator of Design, Art Institute of Chicago. In conversation with the author, February 2010.
103	Julia Lohmann & Gero Grundmann, designers, London. In conversation with the author, February 2010.
104	Michael Smith, collector, London. In conversation with the author, February 2010.
105	Murray Moss, Moss, New York. In conversation with the author, February 2010.
106	Lina Kanafani, Mint, London. In correspondence with the author, March 2010.
107	Emily King, design historian, London. In conversation with the author, February 2010.
108	Arik Levy, designer, Paris. In conversation with the author, February 2010.
109	Janice Blackburn, curator, London. In conversation with the author, February 2010.
110	Maarten Baas, designer. In conversation with the author, February 2010.
111	Gareth Williams, Senior Tutor of Design Products at the RCA, formerly Curator of 20th-century and contemporary furniture at the V&A, London. In conversation with the author, February 2010.
112	Matthew Hilton, designer, London. Quoted in Sophie Lovell, *Limited Edition* (Basel: Birkhäuser, 2009), pp. 76–7.
113	Steve Gourley, MOMART, London; Cliff Williams, Williams & Hill. In email correspondence with the author, March 2010.
114	Steve Gourley, MOMART, London. In email correspondence with the author, March 2010.
115	Sandra Smith, head of conservation at the V&A, London. In correspondence with the author, March 2010.
116	Sandra Smith, head of conservation at the V&A, London. In correspondence with the author, March 2010; vam.ac.uk/res_cons/conservation/index.html.
117	Michael Smith, collector, London. In conversation with the author, February 2010.
118	Sourced from Jack Swabey; Steve Gourley, MOMART, London; Elena Carofyllakis and Adam Prideaux at Heath Lambert/Blackwall Green insurers. In correspondence with the author, March 2010.
119	Sourced from conversations with Sandra Smith, head of conservation, V&A, London; vam.ac.uk; tate.org.uk; Institute of Conservation [ICON]; International Institute for Conservation of Historic and Artistic Works [IIC].
120	Zoë Ryan, Neville Bryan Curator of Design, Art Institute of Chicago. In conversation with the author, February 2010.
121	'Guide for Prospective Buyers', Phillips de Pury Design catalogue, 30 April 2009.
122	Sandra Smith, head of conservation at the V&A, London. In correspondence with the author, March 2010.
123	Adam Lindemann, author and collector, New York. 'Go Ask Adam', in *Art+Auction* April 2009.
124	James Zemaitis, director of 20th-century design, Sotheby's. In conversation with the author, March 2010.

BIBLIOGRAPHY

International design periodicals, including but not limited to *Art+Auction*, *Artnews*, *Art Review*, *Blueprint*, *Frieze*, *Icon* and *Wallpaper**, as well as auction catalogues published since 2002, were consulted for this publication in addition to the following books and exhibition catalogues.

Books:
Jean Baudrillard, *The System of Objects*, trans. James Benedict (London: Verso, 1996).
Walter Benjamin, *Illuminations*, ed. Hannah Arendt, trans. Harry Zohn (London: Pimlico, 1999).
Louisa Buck and Judith Greer, *Owning Art: The Contemporary Art Collector's Handbook* (London: Cultureshock Media, 2006).
Nigel Coates, 'Street Signs', in *Design After Modernism: Beyond the Object*, ed. John Thackara (London: Thames & Hudson, 1988).
Alex Coles, *Design Art: On Art's Romance with Design*, (London: Tate Publishing, 2005).
Charlotte Fiell and Peter Fiell, *Design Now!* (Cologne: Taschen Verlag, 2007).
Adrian Forty, *Objects of Desire: Design and Society since 1750*, (London: Thames & Hudson, 1986).
Philippe Garner, *Eileen Gray: Designer and Architect* (Cologne: Taschen Verlag, 1993).
Sophie Lovell, *Limited Edition: Prototypes, One-Offs and Design Art Furniture* (Basel: Birkhäuser, 2009).
Bruno Munari, *Design as Art*, trans. Patrick Creagh (London: Penguin Books, 1966).
Susan Pearce, *On Collecting: An Investigation into Collecting in the European Tradition* (Oxon: Routledge, 1995).
Alice Rawsthorn, *Marc Newson* (London: Booth Clibborn Editions, 1999).
Penny Sparke, *The Genius of Design* (London: Quadrille Publishing, 2009).
Gareth Williams, *The Furniture Machine: Furniture since 1990* (London: V&A Publications, 2006).
The National Trust Manual of Housekeeping: The Care of Collections in Historic Houses Open to the Public (Oxford: Elsevier Butterworth-Heinemann, 2006).

Exhibition Catalogues:
16 New Pieces, Galerie Kreo (September 2008).
Design and the Elastic Mind (New York: The Museum of Modern Art, 2008).
Design Miami/Basel (June 2007).
Telling Tales: Fantasy and Fear in Contemporary Design (London: V&A Publishing, 2009).

PHOTO CREDITS

All works are © the designers unless otherwise stated; all images are copyright and courtesy of the designers and their studios unless otherwise stated. Photographs in the Timeline are listed separately. Page numbers for the photographs are given in bold.

16 Jean Prouvé (1901–84), Amphitheatre banquette, 1953, Faculté de lettres, Besançon, France, Photograph © 2010. BI, ADAGP, Paris/Scala, Florence/ADAGP, Paris, and DACS, London; **29** Charlotte Perriand (1903–99), Le Corbusier (Charles-Édouard Jeanneret-Gris, 1887–1965) & Pierre Jeanneret (1896–1967), B306 Chaise longue (LC 4), 1928, Photographie FLC L1(20)17, Courtesy Fondation Le Corbusier, © FLC/ADAGP, Paris, and DACS, London; **31** Eileen Gray (1879–1976), Dragon chair, 1917–19, Photograph © Christie's Images, Courtesy Fondation Pierre Bergé Yves Saint Laurent; **33** Charles Eames (1907–78) and Ray Eames (1912–88), Leg splint, 1942, New York, The Museum of Modern Art (MoMA), Gift of the designer, Acc.n.: SC24.1950.1, Photograph © 2010 The Museum of Modern Art, New York/SCALA, Florence; **35** Charles Eames (1907–78) and Ray Eames (1912–88), La Chaise, 1948, Photograph © Bettmann/Corbis; **45** George Nakashima (1905–90), Conoid bench, 1966, Photograph courtesy Dylan Vitone;; **46** Nacho Carbonell (b. 1980), Diversity 18, 2010, Photograph © Tatiana Uzlova/ Galleria Rossana Orlandi, Courtesy Nacho Carbonell **47** Ron Arad (b. 1951), Concrete stereo, 1983; **49** Hella Jongerius (b. 1963), B-Set bowls (for Royal Tichelaar Makkum), 1988; **53** Tord Boontje (b. 1968), Fig-Leaf wardrobe, 2008; **57** Poul Kjaerholm (1929–80), Lounge chair model no. PK 0, designed 1952, executed 1997, Manufactured by Fritz Hansen, Denmark, Photograph courtesy Phillips de Pury; **62 & 63** Maarten Baas (b. 1978), Smoke armchair and chandelier, 2002 (issued 2004), Manufactured by Moooi, Courtesy Moooi; **64** Gerrit Rietveld (1888–1964), Red-and-blue chair, c. 1918, New York, The Museum of Modern Art (MoMA), Gift of Philip Johnson, 487.1953, Photograph © 2010 The Museum of Modern Art, New York/SCALA, Florence, © DACS 2010; **65** Maarten Baas (b. 1978), Where There's Smoke/Red-and-blue chair (Rietveld), 2004, Photograph © Maarten van Houten, Courtesy Marten Baas; **66** Gerrit Rietveld (1888–1964), Zig Zag chair, 1939, New York, Museum of Modern Art (MoMA) Arthur Drexler Fund, Acc.n.: 405.1988, Photograph © 2010 The Museum of Modern Art, New York/SCALA, Florence, © DACS 2010; **67** Maarten Baas (b. 1978), Where There's Smoke/Zig Zag chair (Rietveld), 2002, Photograph © Maarten van Houten, Courtesy Martin Baas; **68** Ettore Sottsass (1917–2007), Carlton divider shelf, 1981, Photograph © 2010 DeAgostini Picture Library/SCALA, Florence; **69** Maarten Baas (b. 1978), Where There's Smoke/Carlton divider shelf (Sottsass), 2004, Photograph © Bas Princen, Courtesy Maarten Baas; **89** Marc Newson (b. 1963), Carbon ladder, 2008, Photograph © Fabrice Gousset, Courtesy Galerie Kreo; **90** Nendo (2002–, Oki Sato, b. 1977), Diamond chair, 2008, Photograph © Masayuki Hayashi, Courtesy Nendo; **91** Barber Osgerby (1996–, Edward Barber, b. 1969, & Jay Osgerby, b. 1969), Iris table, 2008; **92** Jeroen Verhoeven (b. 1980), Cinderella table, 2005, Photograph © Raoul Kramer, Courtesy Studio Demakersvan; **93** Michael Eden (b. 1955), The Wedgwoodn't tureen (tall pink), 2009, London, Crafts Council, acquired 2010, Collection reference: P491, Photograph courtesy Adrian Sassoon; **94** Chris Kabel (b. 1975), Seam chair, 2007; **96** Ron Arad (b. 1951), Rover chair, 1981, Photograph courtesy Phillips de Pury; **97** Tom Dixon (b. 1959), Victorian chair, 1985,

Photograph © Tom Mannion, Courtesy Tom Dixon; **98** Tejo Remy (b. 1960), You Can't Lay Down Your Memory chest of drawers, 1991, Photograph © Gerard van Hees, Courtesy Droog; **99** Fernando (b. 1961) and Humberto Campana (b. 1953), Favela chair, 2003, Manufactured by Edra, Italy, Photograph courtesy Moss; **100** Committee (2001–, Clare Page, b. 1975, & Harry Richardson, b. 1975), Big Brother, 2005; **101** Stuart Haygarth (b. 1966), Tide, 2005; **102** Martino Gamper (b. 1971), If Giò only knew, 2007, Giò Ponti Furniture Courtesy Nilufar Gallery, Milano, Photograph © Emilio Tremolada, courtesy Martino Gamper; **103** Martino Gamper (b. 1971), 100 chairs 100 days, 2007; **104** Rolf Sachs (b. 1955), Tailor Made, 2008, Photograph © Bryon Slater, Courtesy Luchford APM; **105** Liliana Ovalle (b. 1977), Mugroso, 2009; **107** Martí Guixé (b. 1964), Skip furniture, 2004, Photograph © Imagekontainer/Knölke; **108** Dunne & Raby (1994–, Anthony Dunne, b. 1964, & Fiona Raby, b. 1963) with Michael Anastassiades (b. 1967), Priscila Huggable Atomic Mushroom, 2004, Photograph © Francis Ware, Courtesy Dunne & Raby; **109** Gruppo Strum (Giorgio Cerretti, Pietro Derossi, Carlo Gianmarco, Riccardo Rosso and Maurizio Vogliazzo), Pratone seating, 1966–70, Photograph courtesy Gufram; **110** Alessandro Mendini (b. 1931), Proust armchair, 1978, Manufactured by Studio Alchimia, Italy, Museum of Fine Arts, Boston, gift of Mrs S.M.B. Roby and Samuel Putnam Avery Fund, by exchange, 1995.10, Photograph © 2010 Museum of Fine Arts, Boston; **111** Studio Makkink & Bey (2002–, Rianne Makkink, b. 1964, & Jurgen Bey, b. 1965), PROOFF Earchair, 2008, Photograph © Prooff, Courtesy Organisation in Design/Studio Makkink & Bey; **112** Studio Makkink and Bey, (2002–, Rianne Makkink, b. 1964, & Jurgen Bey, b. 1965), Crate cabinets, 2008, Photograph © Bob Goedewaagen, Courtesy Organisation in Design/Studio Makkink & Bey; **113** WOKmedia (2004–, Julie Mathias, b. 1978, & Wolfgang Kaeppner, b. 1974), Once, 2008; **115** Max Lamb (b. 1980), Pewter stool, 2006, Photographs © Jane Lamb and Max Lamb; **116–17** Maarten Baas (b. 1978), Real Time, 2009–10, Photographs © Ricardo sà da Costa, Courtesy Maarten Baas; **118** Atelier NL (2006–, Nadine Sterk, b. 1977, & Lonny van Ryswyck, b. 1978), Sleeping Beauty, 2006, Photograph © Paul Scala, Courtesy Atelier NL; **119** Studio Glithero (2008–, Tim Simpson & Sarah van Gameren), Panta Rei/ Everything Flows, 2008; **120** Studio Glithero (2008–, Tim Simpson & Sarah van Gameren), Running Mould, 2010; **121** Front (2004–, Sofia Lagerkvist, b. 1976, Charlotte von der Lancken, b. 1978, Anna Lindgren, b. 1977, Katja Savstrom, b. 1976), Sketch furniture, 2005, Photographs © Friedman Benda Gallery, Courtesy Front; **122** rAndom International (2002–, Stuart Wood, b.1980, Flo Ortkrass, b. 1976, Hannes Koch, b. 1975) with Chris O'Shea (b. 1981), Audience, 2008, photographed at Basel, 2009; **123** Paul Cocksedge (b. 1978), Kiss, 2009, Photograph © Mark Cocksedge; **124** Julia Lohmann (b. 1977) & Gero Grundmann (b. 1977), Erosion armchair, 2007, Photograph courtesy Gallery Libby Sellers; **125** Frank Tjepkema (b. 1978) and Peter Van der Jagt (b. 1971) for Droog, Do Break, 2000, Photograph © Bianca Pilet, Courtesy Tjep.; **127** Frank O. Gehry (b. 1929), Easy Edges Cardboard Furniture 1969–73, Easy Edges Wiggle side chair, 1971, Photograph courtesy Gehry Partners LLP; **128** Tokujin Yoshioka (b. 1967), Honey Pop, 2001; **129** Tokujin Yoshioka (b. 1967), Venus Natural chair, 2008, Photograph © Masaya Yoshimura; **130** Studio Libertiny (Tomáš Gabzdil Libertiny, b. 1979) , Honeycomb vase, Made by Bees, 2006, Photograph © Raoul Kramer, Courtesy Studio Libertiny; **131** Joris Laarman (b. 1979), Bone chair, 2010, Photograph © Jon Lam, NYC, Courtesy Droog and Friedman

Benda, New York; **132** Arik Levy (b. 1963), Rockshelf and Rocksplit, 2009, Courtesy HSBC Private Bank; **133** Simon Heijdens (b. 1978), Lightweeds, 2006, New York, Museum of Modern Art (MoMA), Photographed at National Gymnasium Tokyo, Japan, 2007, Courtesy Simon Heijdens; **134** Julia Lohmann (b. 1977), Ruminant Bloom, 2004; **135** Ayala Serfaty (b. 1962), Soma, 2009, Photograph © Albi Serfaty, Courtesy Cristina Grajales, Inc.; **137** Gaetano Pesce (b. 1939), Nobody's Perfect, 2002; **138** Kram/Weisshaar (2002–, Reed Kram, b. 1971, & Clemens Weisshaar, b. 1977), Breeding tables, 2003 ongoing, Photograph © Frank Stolle, Courtesy Kram/Weisshaar; **139** Hella Jongerius (b. 1963), Soft urns, 1994, Photograph courtesy Phillips de Pury; **140** Simon Heijdens (b. 1978), Broken White, 2004, Collection Fonds National d'Art Contemporain, France, Courtesy Simon Heijdens; **141** Bertjan Pot (b. 1975), Duct Tape carpet, 2009; **143** Ronan (b. 1971) and Erwan Bouroullec (b. 1976), Lit Clos, 2000, Photograph © Marc Domage, Courtesy Galerie Kreo, Paris; **144** Fredrikson/Stallard (2002–, Patrick Fredrikson, b. 1968, & Ian Stallard, b. 1973), Pyrenees sofa, 2007, Photograph © Thomas Brown, Courtesy David Gill Galleries; **145** Léon de Lange, Karakters, 2008, Photograph © Astrid Zuidena; **146** Lotty Lindeman (b. 1980), Tassenkast, 2009, Courtesy Lotty Lindeman/ Priveekollektie Contemporary Art; **147** Ronan (b. 1971) and Erwan Bouroullec (b. 1976), Lianes, 2010, Photograph © Paul Tahon, Courtesy Galerie Kreo; **153** Marc Newson in his studio, c.1986, Courtesy Marc Newson Ltd; Marc Newson (b.1963), Lockheed Lounge (Edition: Pod), 1986, Photograph © Carin Katt, Photograph courtesy Phillips de Pury.

DESIGN TIMELINE

Numbers here refer to illustration numbers on pages 72 to 83.

1 A. W. N. Pugin (1812–52), attr., early Victorian oak three-leaf screen, c. 1850, Photograph © Christie's Images Limited 2010; **2** Charles Rennie Mackintosh (1828–1968), Ladderback chairs, c. 1903, Private collection, Photograph © The Fine Art Society, London, UK/ The Bridgeman Art Library; **3** Gerrit Rietveld (1888–1964), Red-and-blue chair, c. 1918, New York, The Museum of Modern Art (MoMA), Gift of Philip Johnson, 487.1953, Photograph © 2010 The Museum of Modern Art, New York/SCALA, Florence, © DACS 2010; **4** Eileen Gray (1879–1976), Screen, 1922, New York, Museum of Modern Art (MoMA), Guimard Fund, Acc. n.: 476.1978, Photograph © 2010 The Museum of Modern Art, New York/ SCALA, Florence, © Prunella Clough; **5** Marcel Breuer (1902–81), Club chair B3 (Wassily), 1925, Private collection, Photograph © The Bridgeman Art Library; **6** Emile-Jacques Ruhlmann (1879–1933), Cabanel Chiffonier, c. 1921–22, Photograph courtesy Sotheby's New York; **7** Ludwig Mies van der Rohe (1886–1969), Barcelona model MR 90 chair, 1929, Museum of Fine Arts, Houston, Texas, USA, Museum purchase with funds from by J. Brian and Varina Eby, Photograph © Museum of Fine Arts, Houston/ The Bridgeman Art Library, © DACS 2010; **8** Jean Royère (1902–81), Armchair, c. 1936, Manufactured by Gouffé, France, Photograph courtesy Phillips de Pury; **9** Alvar Aalto (1898–1976), Paimio armchair, 1930, Photograph © V&A Images/Victoria and Albert Museum; **10** Hans Wegner (1914–2007), Dolphin chair, c. 1950, Produced by Johannes Hansen, Denmark, Photograph courtesy Phillips de Pury; **11** Alexandre Noll (1890–1970), Dining table, c. 1950, Photograph courtesy Phillips de Pury; **12** Serge Mouille (1922–88), Two-arm wall light, c. 1954, Manufactured by Ateliers Serge Mouille, France, Photograph courtesy Phillips de Pury; **13** Giò Ponti (1891–1979), Superleggera side chair, 1951, New York, Museum of Modern Art (MoMA), Gift of the manufacturer, SC2.1953, Photograph © 2010 The Museum of Modern Art, New York/SCALA, Florence; **14** Achille (1918–2002) and Pier Giacomo Castiglioni (1913–68), Mezzadro stool, 1957, Photograph © 2010 DeAgostini Picture Library/SCALA, Florence **15** Pierre Jeanneret (1896–1967), Illuminated library table, from Chandigarh, India, c. 1966, Photograph courtesy Phillips de Pury, © ADAGP, Paris, and DACS, London, 2010; **16** Superstudio (1966–82, Adolfo Natalini, b.1941, & Cristiano Toraldo di Francia, b. 1941), Bazaar seating environment, 1968, Manufactured by Giovanetti, Italy, Photograph courtesy Phillips de Pury; **17** Gaetano Pesce (b. 1939), Donna Up5 chair, 1969; **18** Wendell Castle (b. 1932), Crescent Rocker, 1982, Photograph courtesy Wright; **19** Gino Sarfatti (1912–85), Floor lamp, c. 1971, Manufactured by Arteluce, Italy, Photograph courtesy Phillips de Pury; **20** Joe Colombo (1930–71), Tube chair, c. 1970, Manufactured by Flexform, Photograph courtesy Phillips de Pury; **21** Ettore Sottsass (1917–2007), Biedermeier sofa, 1982, Photograph courtesy Phillips de Pury; **22** Ron Arad (b. 1951), Big Easy chair, 1988; **23** Elizabeth Garouste (b. 1949) and Mattia Bonetti (b. 1953), Prince Imperial chair, c. 1985, Photograph courtesy Sotheby's New York, © ADAGP, Paris, and DACS, London, 2010; **24** Shiro Kuramata (1934–91), How High the Moon chair, c. 1986, Manufactured by Terada Tekkojo, Japan, Photograph courtesy Phillips de Pury; **25** Jasper Morrison (b. 1959), Ply chair and Ply table, 1988, Photograph courtesy Phillips de Pury; **26** Philippe Starck (b. 1949), Juicy Salif citrus-squeezer, 1990, Photograph courtesy Alessi S.p.a., Crusinallo, Italy; **27** Tejo Remy (1960–), You Can't Lay Down Your Memory chest of drawers, 1991, Photograph © Gerard van Hees, Courtesy Droog; **28** Tom Dixon (b. 1959), Jack light, 1997, re-released 2010, Photograph © Tom Mannion, Courtesy Tom Dixon; **29** Fernando (b. 1961) and Humberto Campana (b. 1953), Banquet chair, 2007, Courtesy Moss; **30** Atelier Van Lieshout (1995–, Joep van Lieshout, b. 1963), Prick floor lamp, 2004, Photograph courtesy Phillips de Pury; **31** Zaha Hadid (b. 1950), Aqua table, 2005, Photograph © Peter Guenzel, Courtesy Established & Sons; **32** Studio Job (1998–, Job Smeets, b. 1970, & Nynke Tynagel, b. 1977, 2000–), Robber Baron jewel safe, 2006; **33** Marc Newson (b. 1963), Voronoi shelf, 2007; **34** Martino Gamper (b. 1971), Total Trattoria, 2008, Photograph © Shira Klasmer, Courtesy Martino Gamper **35** Konstantin Grcic (b. 1965), Karbon Chaise, 2008, Photograph © Fabrice Gousset, Courtesy Galerie Kreo; **36** Fredrikson/Stallard (Patrick Fredrikson, b. 1968, & Ian Stallard, b. 1973), Gasoline garden vase: Cadillac, 2009, Photograph © Thomas Brown, Courtesy David Gill Gallery.